DOUBTLESS

Because Faith Is Hard

SHELBY ABBOTT

New Growth Press, Greensboro, NC 27404
newgrowthpress.com

All of the names used in this book have been changed for privacy.

Cover Design: Faceout Books, faceoutstudio.com
Interior Design and Typesetting: Gretchen Logterman

ISBN: 978-1-64507-075-7 (Print)
ISBN: 978-1-64507-092-4 (eBook)

Library of Congress Cataloging-in-Publication Data
Names: Abbott, Shelby, 1977- author.
Title: Doubtless : because faith is hard / Shelby Abbott.
Description: Greensboro, NC : New Growth Press, 2020. | Includes bibliographical references. | Summary: "Is God good? Can I trust him with my life? Is the Bible true? These are just some of the questions that can plague young adults as they stand at the crossroads of life. Shelby Abbott comes alongside young adults to help them honestly face their misgivings and turn to God for the gift of faith, encouraging them to see the difference between doubt and unbelief. DoubtLess is full of gospel hope for those grappling with the mysteries of faith"-- Provided by publisher.
Identifiers: LCCN 2020010219 (print) | LCCN 2020010220 (ebook) | ISBN 9781645070757 (trade paperback) | ISBN 9781645070924 (ebook)
Subjects: LCSH: Faith. | Trust in God--Christianity. | Christian youth--Religious life.
Classification: LCC BV4637 .A26 2020 (print) | LCC BV4637 (ebook) | DDC 234/.23--dc23
LC record available at https://lccn.loc.gov/2020010219
LC ebook record available at https://lccn.loc.gov/2020010220

Printed in The United States of America

27 26 25 24 23 22 21 20 1 2 3 4 5

"Shelby Abbott brings years of ministry experience and wisdom to this book and provides a path forward when we experience doubt in our walk with Jesus. We learn to feed our faith, focus on the foundations of God's Word and the resurrection of Christ, and move from cynicism to trust. This exceptional and beautifully written book invites us to work through—not wallow in—our questions and doubts in a mature and productive way."

Heather Holleman, Speaker; author of *Seated with Christ: Living Freely in a Culture of Comparison* and *Sent: Living a Life that Invites Others to Jesus*

"How should we respond to those in our day who celebrate skepticism and suggest that having doubts about your faith is somehow a virtue or a hallmark of genuine spiritual enlightenment? We should respond as my friend Shelby Abbott has done masterfully in this important book. This will be a needed lifeline for so many."

Bob Lepine, Cohost, FamilyLife Today radio

"If you think about it, doubt has a significant social dimension—a badge of authenticity to brag or post about, an isolating struggle to keep hidden from others, a stigmatizing mark of spiritual weakness or immaturity, or an affirmation of personal courage and individualism. *DoubtLess* is, to my knowledge, the only book on the subject that speaks to this social dimension, and what is unique about doubt in a digital age. I could not recommend the book more highly, nor Shelby Abbott as the person to engage the subject—he's safe, affirming, humble, empathetic, honest, and above all, biblical in his counsel."

Rick James, Publisher, Cru Press

"Shelby Abbott has taken something with the power to thwart the growth of Christians and tamed it into submission. His honest and sympathetic words on the subject of doubt reveal a depth of understanding that can only come through experience. Abbott shows us that it's easier to overcome doubt when it's not viewed as a powerful monster, and in *Doubtless* he slays the dragon; not through apologetics so much as through the love and mercy of God."

Katherine James, Author of *Can You See Anything Now?* and *A Prayer for Orion*

"Doubt is not a word we want to be associated with our faith. Doubting God can feel shameful and even sinful. *DoubtLess* does the important work of meeting us in our questions and teaching us how to honestly bring them to God and fellow Christians. In the process, we learn that humbly wrestling with our questions is essential to developing a mature, discerning, and persevering faith. In these pages, Shelby provides the gentle shepherding we need to lean upon God, even when we're tempted to doubt him."

Garrett Kell, Pastor, Del Ray Baptist Church, Alexandria, VA

"It's time that we bring doubt out of the closet of shame, and fear of man into the shining light of the wisdom of God's Word and beautiful grace. This is exactly what *DoubtLess* does. Here is ancient truth communicated and applied in winsome and fresh new ways. Since doubt is a tool God regularly uses to strengthen our faith and draw us closer to him, I can't think of anyone who wouldn't benefit from *DoubtLess*, which helps us face our struggles of faith in the presence of our patient and loving Lord. This is a really needed and very good book."

Paul David Tripp, Pastor; author; international conference speaker

"With over two decades of experience in meaningful relationships with the rising generation, Shelby Abbott guides you through an honest and healthy space to process doubt and questions, while seeking answers and authentic faith formation."

David Robbins, President, FamilyLife

"When it comes to conveying gospel truth to young adults, Shelby Abbott is one of the most trustworthy and effective voices I know."

Matt Smethurst, Managing Editor, The Gospel Coalition; author of *Before You Open Your Bible: Nine Heart Postures for Approaching God's Word*

"Shelby Abbott has given the body of Christ a great gift by writing this book. He has given us a practical resource that encourages the doubting Christian to confront, lean in to, and walk through their doubts. In each chapter, he digs beneath the surface, helping to navigate the reasons why we doubt, while offering healthy ways to address the issues that lead to a faltering faith—ultimately encouraging the Christian to keep their eyes fixed on the author and perfecter of our faith, Jesus Christ. Wildly encouraging!"

Alisa Childers, Speaker; author of *Another Gospel: A Lifelong Christian Seeks Truth in Response to Progressive Christianity*

Contents

For Drew.

Foreword

I was a student twice, and both times I could have really used this book.

The first time, I was a brand-new believer. I had come to Christ just a matter of months earlier. A whole new reality had opened up to me. I knew my Creator. I loved the Scriptures. I found refreshment and joy in church. But all this very nearly came crashing down around me. The first week of my studies I was told by my professors in no uncertain terms that if, by the time I graduated, I still believed what I was professing to believe at that moment, they would consider themselves to have failed. They nearly succeeded. My faith in Christ was assaulted from all academic directions. It nearly overwhelmed me.

Thankfully, a godly pastor came alongside and helped me think through the challenges I was facing. He provided endless safety and time. He also showed me that much of what I was being taught in the classroom was just one side of various arguments to which Christians had found compelling answers. I almost always ended up doing twice as much reading as my fellow students: the materials assigned by the professor, and then those my pastor directed my way. It was heavy, intense work, but it helped me examine what I was taught from every possible angle.

However, this caused problems a few years later, when I became a student at another school in a different city. This time it wasn't my studies that was the issue—it was my new pastor. I'd been told that this church had solid, biblical teaching, and it did—kind of. The problem was, most major questions were out of bounds. We were told *what* to think and *what* to believe, but never *how* to think and *how* to believe. Curiosity was dismissed as a distraction. Uncertainty was seen as disloyalty. So I came along, always wanting to question, reexamine, and pull apart what I was being told to see if it really stood up to scrutiny—and was quickly made to feel as if I was a stumbling block to everyone else.

That's why I wish Shelby had been around twenty years ago. For starters, it would have been great fun; I can't spend more than a moment in his company without the two of us laughing hysterically at something. But it would also have been reassuring. Shelby, like that first pastor I had, would have been a steady guide through choppy academic waters. And, unlike that second pastor, he would also have embraced the need to ask real questions and express real uncertainties.

What it comes down to is this: if Christianity can't be questioned, it isn't worth believing. More than that: not only can Christianity withstand our doubts and uncertainties, there's a real sense in which bringing them to the table actually dignifies the claims of Christ. He can take it. And he invites it. Our faith will be the stronger and more compelling for it. I'd go as far as saying that the doubts I had back then are what has trained me to be an apologist now.

But don't take my word for it. Dive into this book. You won't regret it.

Sam Allberry, Senior Apologist, Ravi Zacharias International Ministries; author

Introduction

Faith is a wrestle with doubt.
—Martin Luther

I sat across the room from Ben and Kyle during the summer after their freshman year of college and tried to listen intently to the noticeably uncomfortable questions they had in regard to their faith. Both of these young men were bright and thoughtful, and when they communicated their concerns about God, Jesus, faith, and commitment, they did so without a hint of cynicism. They genuinely wanted to know my thoughts on a variety of belief-based subjects.

I've been a full-time missionary working with college students for more than twenty years. During our conversation, my experience helped me to frequently ask clarifying questions that dug deeper into the reasons behind their obvious doubts, while trying to steer clear of any specific platitudes that might cause them to roll their eyes and dismiss me altogether. They had been routinely challenged by their professors in their first year of college to call into question the existence of God, along with the belief that Jesus was the Savior of all mankind. Needless to say, the constant challenging had taken its toll.

"How can I be sure that God is real? And if he is, why does he let so many horrible things happen every day?" Kyle asked me.

"Yeah, and aren't there a ton of errors in the Bible? How can we trust that it is actually the Word of God?" Ben questioned, cutting in before I could even open my mouth.

See, Ben and Kyle were two Christian college students who attended a secular university in Pittsburgh. They were talking with me that day because they had been accepted to a ten-week summer mission I run in Ocean City, Maryland—and their questions came after only one week in Ocean City. Some of their professors had planted the seeds of doubt in their minds and they were clearly struggling with their faith. They were curious about what that meant for their future not only for the rest of the summer, but as believers in Christ in the coming years of school.

My constant temptation was to refute the things their university instructors had stated, point by point, and in a sense "win" any arguments between me and the other people who weren't even in the room. But by God's grace—and despite the fact that I was incredibly angry at each of their professors for the amount of distress they had caused these guys—I was able to resist that temptation.

In the end, I applauded both of the students for seeking truth and honestly inquiring about a belief system that, if true, demands our total allegiance and devotion (1 Corinthians 7:22–23; Ephesians 6:6). I typed up a resource guide for each of them to check out and encouraged them to read about our faith. I told them that they shouldn't be ashamed about their doubt—but stressed that where doubt had the ability to lead was, spiritually speaking, a matter of life and death.

Doubt Defined

It's important to understand what doubt actually is and what it isn't before making assumptions on the nature of what we'll be talking about in the coming chapters. Many people, Christians in particular, conclude that doubt is the same thing as unbelief. Let me assure you that it's not.

If doubt were the same as unbelief, I don't know a single follower of Christ who could be certain that their salvation was secure. They would feel as if their eternal destiny were in the throes of a cosmic ping-pong match, bouncing back and forth between heaven and hell, peace and anxiety, joy and despair. Unbelief is a conclusion someone reaches—a deliberate decision to live life as if there is no God. Doubt is something significantly different.

It's natural for questions about our faith to develop when life gets confusing or difficult. Skepticism and qualms have certainly been common in my many years of following Christ. But let's not confuse our questions or hesitations of certainty with confident conclusions about rejecting faith—they're not the same thing. Doubt is what Alister McGrath calls, "A wistful longing to be sure of the things in which we trust."[1] By its own nature, it arises within the context of faith, directly implying that doubt and faith are two things that can coexist in someone's life at the same time. To say that doubt and unbelief are the same is tantamount to saying temptation is the same as sin. They're not equivalent to one another, no matter how similar they might seem.

However, just as sin can creep in during moments of temptation, unbelief can be born amid doubt. Like a child who constantly seeks the attention of his mom and dad, doubt demands more attention the longer you pay attention to it, and it can easily transform into something much uglier. I'm not saying it's harmful to pay attention to our doubts (otherwise, I wouldn't have written this book), but there's a specific difference between addressing our doubts and celebrating them. An intentional celebration of doubt can quickly backslide into a glorification of it, so it's crucial we approach our doubts with discernment.

We must recognize the distinct difference between doubt and unbelief, but at the same time understand that the former can easily lead to the latter if we obsess over it. This is key as we begin, because to really grasp our struggle and start to see victory we need to clearly comprehend doubt for what it is and what it's not.

Your Unique Complexity

As a young person in our culture today, whether you're a student or newly in the workforce, you face opposition to your faith in a unique way, one that can raise up ample amounts of doubt. If you're in high school or college, at almost no other point in your life will you be in an environment that encourages deep thought, intentional study, and challenging opinions—all within the context of a community of your peers doing the exact same things. High school and college are settings that encourage you to question the status quo; however, keep in mind that your encouragement itself is coming from a partisan viewpoint. While asking questions is great for growing and developing (most of the time), it can also be damaging if you aren't careful.

Let me explain. If you're a student, you need to be prepared for the biased opinions of your teachers, professors, and the secular learning environment at large, even if they happen to be teaching the Bible in something like a Religion 101 class. Those who teach aren't neutral, and to believe they are without opinion and just stating "the facts" in a classroom can be naïve. Michael Kruger, president and a professor of New Testament and early Christianity at Reformed Theological Seminary, puts it well when he says, "We have this mentality that professors are walking around in a white lab coat, objectively looking at things from a neutral and unbiased perspective, but that is not true. They've been trained at a secular university to look at the Bible from a secular standpoint, and they are going to teach from that standpoint . . . in a biased way."[2]

So yes, you are being taught to think deeply, but that teaching applies to how you approach a lot of important topics. And as a result, the lessons from the front of the classroom can come in direct conflict with your Christian faith, possibly dropping you into a shadowy valley of doubt and discouragement.

Not only that, but the gospel itself will most likely be intentionally ignored or purposefully challenged at every angle while you are a student or in the workforce. In our current culture,

Christianity is frequently written off as close-minded and archaic, with its belief system now on the "wrong side of history." To communicate with someone that, because of our sin, we are separated from an eternal God who loves and created humanity, and that the only way to reconcile with him is by allowing the sacrificial blood of his Son Jesus Christ to pay the penalty for that sin, making him the Master and Savior of your life, is indeed countercultural. More than likely, you will be marginalized for voicing your allegiance to Christ in the context of the classroom at a secular university or within the workplace.

Mature Discernment

That said, I believe it's important to have a healthy and realistic approach when it comes to the subject of doubt. If we ignore it when it shows up, it can fester and become quite dangerous. Conversely, if we feed it and become constantly preoccupied by it, doubt can pose a real threat by growing into the primary topic on which our heart dwells.

We need to approach doubt with a mature level of discernment. This book is designed to give you the tools to develop a healthy sense of godly perception when doubt hits. Together we will walk through various aspects of what it means to grapple with doubt as a young person, and how to address our longing to be certain in light of the gospel.

I've been in full-time missions work with students since I graduated from college. From where I stand, it's not really a matter of *if* you will wrestle with doubt but *when*. Consequently, it's a subject that needs to be discussed in a safe environment of grace, truth, and love. My prayer is that this book will foster that kind of atmosphere in your heart and among the people with whom you trust to share your struggles.

I think also it's important to note that this book will not address apologetics (defense of the Christian faith) per se. There are countless books and resources that are extremely valuable when it comes to sound arguments on behalf of Christianity (see some of my recommended examples on the "For Further Reading" page at the end of the book). There is no need for me to contribute much in that arena. Instead, I'd like to address the questions *behind* the questions that young people wrestle with on a continual basis *through* their doubt. Questions like:

- What does it mean for my Christianity if I'm doubting?
- Am I all alone in my doubt? Is anyone else doubting too?
- I feel embarrassed, so should I tell people if I'm doubting?
- Is the Bible actually trustworthy?
- I don't feel loved by God right now, so is he really there?
- Why am I so anxious when I have questions and doubts about God?
- Is God really all-powerful? If so, why does it seem like he doesn't care about me or others who suffer?

Among many others, these are the kinds of questions I want to tackle. For the sake of clarity, I've organized the book into two main sections. The first I've labeled "Foundational Doubts." These will tackle the larger struggles one deals with when exploring questions about God and the Christian faith. The second section, "Everyday Doubts," will address more ground-level doubts one can deal with on a day-in day-out basis but doesn't really jostle your faith in the same way foundational doubts can.

When we grapple with the difficulty that comes because of our doubts (whether small or grand), it can feel lonely. But I encourage you to lean into your relationship with God in the process, instead of succumbing to the temptation to flee from him. Let's link arms together and move forward, with a spirit of hope and expectancy, as we trust the Lord during the struggle. May our faith in Jesus Christ be anchored and strengthened through our wrestling with doubt.

SECTION ONE

FOUNDATIONAL DOUBTS

This section will examine many of the major doubts one can have when wrestling with the larger issues of life and faith. Putting our trust in God is hard when the circumstances of our lives don't seem to match up with what Scripture communicates. However, being diligent about the pursuit of truth and our relationship with God is always worth it—because of what's on the line. When foundational doubts arise, I can't think of anything more important than seeking God with consistency and vigor instead of passivity and retreat. I hope this section will help you in the chase as you move forward.

CHAPTER ONE

Doubt Is Biblical and Common

"Why, O Lord, do you stand far away? Why do you hide yourself in times of trouble?"
(Psalm 10:1)

In your current season of life, it's easy to feel shaken by the overabundance of questions you've probably never heard asked before—questions that have either arisen from within you or questions being asked by others around you like classmates, neighbors, or coworkers. Consequently, this is likely the first time you've really had to wrestle with making the Christian faith your own. You might feel confused, skeptical, uneasy, or even anxious about your faith, and all of those experiences are completely new to you.

There is a common school of thought among many in the Christian community that if someone is wrestling with any questions or doubts concerning God, his goodness, his sovereignty, his presence, or any other of his attributes, he or she is immature and not "doing well" in his or her walk with the Lord. While this is sometimes true, it's important not to jump to any conclusions about the state of someone's relationship with God before finding out the facts.

I work for a Christian organization called Cru, and my primary mission field is eighteen- to twenty-eight-year-olds. Naturally, I've been given many opportunities to choose young people to lead various ministry aspects in the effort to help fulfill the Great Commission (Matthew 28:18–20). A few years ago, one such case came up on a staff team I was leading. A college student named Maisie was proposed as the leader of a weekly women's time that about twenty other Christian college women would attend, in order to participate and gain perspective on biblical womanhood. The women's time was to be completely student-led, and Maisie was definitely the kind of leader we needed to shepherd that ministry.

However, during our selection brainstorm, someone on the staff team mentioned that Maisie was working through some doubts she had about God and his goodness. When we all heard this, I, along with many others on the team, confessed that this changed my perspective on her leadership potential, and we began to throw around a few other names to discuss for selection. One of the other Cru staff men stopped us mid-conversation and said, "Wait. Why would the fact that Maisie is wrestling with doubt disqualify her from leading the women's time?"

It was a good question, and one that really made me think for the first time about doubt in a more thorough way. In the past, I believed someone who doubted was spiritually weak and lacked the faith needed to call himself a devoted follower of Christ. In my misguided perspective, I was unable to recall not only the seasons of doubt I had experienced in my own life, but the clear examples of doubt peppered throughout the pages of Scripture as well.

Maisie wasn't a subpar leader because she was wrestling with doubt. If anything, she showed great leadership by being humble enough to make known to other people that she was struggling, and all of us should have seen that.

The Bible helps us clear up the confusion in our encounters with doubt—not only by talking specifically about it but by giving us easy-to-see models who illustrate what someone thinks and says when he or she is doubting.

Doubt Is Common in the Psalms

Let's start with the book of Psalms. After I became a Christian during my freshman year of college, the Psalms were such a comforting oasis of honest poetry to me, because of how raw and candid they were. In the months following my decision for Christ, Psalms was always the book I turned to first when I started my private times with God, simply because I felt like that as I read the Psalms, they were actually reading me.

I loved how "human" they were. I could easily see myself in their words. It was almost as if my reflection could be spotted when the psalm scandalously described frustration, anger, or confusion with God. Psalm 13 (a psalm of David) gives us a good example of what I'm talking about:

> How long, O LORD? Will you forget me forever?
> How long will you hide your face from me?
> How long must I take counsel in my soul
> and have sorrow in my heart all the day?
> How long shall my enemy be exalted over me?
> (Psalm 13:1–2)

In this text, David essentially asks God if he cares at all about David's life. He's questioning God's timing, goodness, and sovereignty, all in two little verses. He takes intentional time to write out the deepest, darkest parts of his thought process for us, in so doing, David becomes a representation for humanity living in a sinful world.

I've certainly asked some of these questions in my mind and heart—maybe not in the same poetic rhetoric of King David, but I've asked them nonetheless. During the most difficult trials of my life, I've prayed, "Where are you, God? Remember me? How long will I have to put up with this misery? When will this pain come to an end?"

And following my hostile questioning, when I've felt the subsequent pang of guilt for doubting God's love during my hurt, reading psalms like this one have always brought me genuine comfort. It's reassuring to know that the guy labeled a "man after [God's] own heart" (1 Samuel 13:14) doubted God in the exact same ways I've doubted him in the past.

Not only is there biblical evidence of doubting God found in one psalm—it's all over the book. Psalm 10:1 asks God why he hides himself in times of trouble. Psalm 22:1–2 (the psalm Jesus quotes while he's being crucified) asks God why he has forsaken David. In Psalm 74:1, Asaph wonders why God has cast him off forever. Psalm 77:7–9 questions whether God's love has forever ceased, and on and on (e.g., Psalm 79:5; 88; 94:19; 137).

The Psalms show each of us that doubt is common. Not only do they give us permission to explore our negative feelings; by example, they almost *force* us to lean into them. I once heard a pastor describe this exploration by saying, "The psalms give us permission to beat on God's chest."[1] The imagery here is dramatic, and it resonates with me because I can imagine crying with my face buried in God's chest, screaming, "Why would you let this happen to me?"

It's easy for me to picture because I already did something like this a few years ago. I suffer from chronic pain due to a herniated disc in my lower back that puts pressure on my sciatic nerve. It's a daily battle for me, and after about three years I remember standing in my bathroom with tears running down my face and my head buried in the towels that hung from the rack. I beat the wall through the towels and audibly said, "Have you even heard anything I've prayed about over the last three years? Where are you, God? Why won't you help me?"

So I get it. And consequently, I like when the Psalms get super-real. It helps to know that I'm in good company when I wrestle with the same kind of doubts that King David had, and struggle with the same questions asked in Psalm 22. Doubt and pain can be incredibly isolating, and the Psalms help us to know we're not alone when we doubt.

Be Honest with God

Evan, a college student I occasionally met with, confessed to me that he was wrestling with doubts about God's existence as a result of his closest friend dying in a car crash. He was angry that

God allowed his friend to die, and as a result wondered if God even existed at all. He felt guilty for pondering these things but his doubts were, all of a sudden, very real. It was like one day Evan was a cheerful Christian who loved God, read his Bible, and shared his faith, and the next day he was seriously questioning the validity of Christianity and God's existence altogether. The burden of faith weighed heavy on Evan's shoulders, and he suddenly believed that life would just be easier if he didn't have the element of faith to lug around with him wherever he went.

I truly felt the anguish Evan was going through, and I remember thanking him for his transparency. One of the worst things he could have done was to hold those feelings and doubts inside him, granting them the opportunity to grow and fester in a way that would eventually become all-consuming.

It reminded me of Habakkuk and his honesty with God during the injustice he witnessed all around him: "O Lord, how long shall I cry for help, and you will not hear? Or cry to you 'Violence!' and you will not save? Why do you make me see iniquity, and why do you idly look at wrong? Destruction and violence are before me; strife and contention arise" (Habakkuk 1:2–3).

I love this because it echoes what I've certainly thought before, and what Evan was talking with me about that day. Habakkuk seems to be saying, "God, you say that you're good and that you listen to the cries of your people, but look around. All the evidence is to the contrary. I doubt your goodness and your personal interest in making wrong things right."

Scripture like this teaches us to be honest with God. In the moment, Habakkuk can't reconcile the world he sees with the good God he knows, so instead of being silent about his doubt he speaks up and talks to God about it. He doesn't let it become an all-encompassing, life-swallowing problem that defines his heart. He engages with God and openly talks with him about his confusion and frustration. He freely dialogues with his heavenly Father and brings his bewilderment to God's feet. And as a result, we find out at the end of Habakkuk 3 that God willingly enters into a conversation with Habakkuk, which draws them closer together and culminates in Habakkuk rejoicing in the Lord despite his circumstances.

Doubt in the New Testament

We don't see doubt happening only in the Old Testament; it's in the New Testament as well. There is an interesting story near the middle of Mark 9 that also addresses the subject of doubt, and this piece of Scripture involves Christ himself:

> And they brought the boy to him. And when the spirit saw him, immediately it convulsed the boy, and he fell on the ground and rolled about, foaming at the mouth. And Jesus asked his father, "How long has this been happening to him?" And he said, "From childhood. And it has often cast him into fire and into water, to destroy him. But if you can do anything, have compassion on us and help us." And Jesus said to him, "'If you can!' All things are possible for one who believes." Immediately the father of the child cried out and said, "I believe; help my unbelief!" And when Jesus saw that a crowd came running together, he rebuked the unclean spirit, saying to it, "You mute and deaf spirit, I command you, come out of him and never enter him again." And after crying out and convulsing him terribly, it came out, and the boy was like a corpse, so that most of them said, "He is dead." But Jesus took him by the hand and lifted him up, and he arose. (Mark 9:20–27)

You'll notice that Jesus doesn't scold the father for his doubt, nor chastise him because he can't completely trust in Jesus's capability of healing his son. When the man brings his demon-possessed child to Jesus and asks him if he can do anything to cast out the unclean spirit, Jesus responds by saying "'If you can'! All things are possible for him who believes" (v. 23). The father of the child then cries out, "I believe; help my unbelief!" (v. 24).

I love the candor of the dad in this story, and I can certainly relate to the fact that he believes yet knows there's also a part of him that doesn't. So instead of pretending he's 100 percent faithful and giving Jesus false lip service about belief, he admits there's an element of doubt in his heart that needs help.

The truly fascinating thing that comes as a result of the dad's honesty is that, if anything, Jesus actually rewards his declaration of doubt. In verses 25–29, we see the story play out with Jesus casting out the demon, the boy looking like he's dead as a result of the exorcism, Jesus taking the boy's hand, lifting him up, and walking alongside him into the house. Just after the boy's father cries out, "Help my unbelief," Jesus performs the miracle and instantly changes both his life and the boy's.

Jesus wasn't turned off by the man's apparent apprehension. This parent needed Christ's help while he wrestled with doubt—and help was, of course, extended to him.

I wonder how often we as Christians take up the kind of posture modeled for us here. I don't know about you, but I often don't have the kind of gracious response that Jesus does when someone is transparent enough to communicate their doubt. More likely, I'm prone to argue with them or silently judge them for not living the life of faith they "should be" living as followers of Christ. This certainly is not the right attitude, but I'm willing to bet I'm not the only ungracious example.

For some reason in our Christian culture today, we are scorned for any signs of doubt we might wrestle with, and vaguely encouraged to "have more faith" when life's challenges beat down hard on us. From what I've seen and experienced, there is little room in campus ministry or church culture for the kind of honesty that unashamedly cries out, "Help my unbelief!"

Yet, the New Testament teems with examples of God's people struggling with doubt in a candid way, which helps us to know our Lord understands and wants to extend his hand to us during the struggle. Jude 22 simply says, "And have mercy on those who doubt," leading us to clearly see that we should respond to people's doubts in a loving and gentle way instead of a negative and judgmental way.

Just as I Am

It's important to note that we should always be authentic with God. He can handle it. He isn't made insecure by our doubts or rattled when we question his methods. We should never feel as if we can't come to God in our worst moments. If we believe that the only times we're allowed to talk to God is when we're doing great—when we're wearing our spiritual Sunday-best clothes, so to speak—we have a biblically inaccurate view of him.

When Jesus died on the cross, he became sin so that we might become pure. Second Corinthians 5:21 states, "For our sake he made him to be sin who knew no sin, so that in him we might become the righteousness of God." This verse is often referred to as "the great exchange," because it tells us that Jesus took all our sin on himself and transferred all of his righteousness onto us. Once we accept the payment he made on the cross, when God looks at us he sees Christ's righteousness. We're freed up entirely to come to God just as we are. Though we may feel dirty, sinful, and unworthy to be honest with God in our moments of doubt (or any moment at all), if we are in Christ, God sees only his Son's perfection and none of the impurities.

Charlotte Elliot suffered from chronic pain, depression, and feelings of uselessness in the 1800s. At one point, she was visited by a clergyman who said to her, "You need to come just as you are to the Lamb of God." She listened but refused his advice until one day, coming to the epiphany that God wasn't in relationship with her because she was useful. She had a breakthrough moment that inspired her to write the world-renowned and beloved hymn, "Just as I Am."[2] The hymn became a staple for hymnals and was widely used as the altar call song for the Billy Graham crusades that started in the late 1940s and ran all the way through 2005.

Charlotte's lyrics became the anthem for doubters everywhere, and an encouragement to men and women who wanted to be honest with God about their doubt. You might be familiar with this hymn already, but take a closer look at the third verse:

> Just as I am, though tossed about
> With many a conflict, many a doubt
> Fightings and fears within, without
> Oh Lamb of God I come, I come.[3]

Charlotte Elliot was familiar with a faith in crisis, and learned that in spite of her doubts she could come to God just as she was because of Christ's atoning sacrifice for her—he wouldn't be turned off by her and her doubt. What a helpful model of a life lived with authenticity.

John the Baptist

I want to wrap up this chapter with just one more clear example of biblical doubt, so we can see what kind of company we keep. John the Baptist was a godly man who was described as "the voice of one crying out in the wilderness, 'Make straight the way of the Lord'" (John 1:23, cf. Isaiah 40:3), because he was the precursor to the Messiah.

At one point, John had directed his own disciples to stop following him and follow after Christ instead, calling Jesus "the Lamb of God, who takes away the sin of the world!" (John 1:29). In light of that, he obviously believed, right? I mean, he made it clear to the people who asked him that he was not the Messiah (John 1:20), and that Jesus was the Christ.

Elsewhere in Scripture, we can see that John the Baptist was the unborn baby who leapt inside his mother's womb at the mere presence of Christ (Luke 1:41). He saw the heavens open above him as the Holy Spirit descended on Jesus after John baptized the Son of God (Matthew 3:13–17). John heard the voice of God say about Jesus, "This is my beloved Son, with whom I am well pleased" (Matthew 3:17). In light of all this evidence, you'd think that John would never have doubted that Jesus was who he said he was—the Savior of the world.

But even John, at one point, had his doubts.

Near the end of his life, we find John in prison facing an imminent death penalty. He calls two of his disciples over and requests that they go to Jesus and ask him, "Are you the one who is to come, or shall we look for another?" (Luke 7:19). John is essentially saying, "I want to believe that you're the One, but right now I'm not sure."[4]

Really? After all he had seen and testified about? After calling Jesus the Lamb of God who takes away the sin of the world? After hearing the audible voice of God the Father call down from heaven that Jesus was his Son? After all that, the precursor to the Messiah himself doubts that Jesus is the actual Messiah?

While all these facts about John the Baptist might make someone scoff at his lack of faith, I'm oddly comforted by his doubt. Why? Because if he could doubt and admit it plainly—to the point that it's recorded in Scripture—I certainly can have the liberty to doubt and be honest about it too. I'm free from the shame of admitting my doubts and now open to honestly walking in my faith, knowing that God is big enough to handle it when I doubt him.

And let's not forget how Jesus himself responded once John's questions were passed along to him: he was patient and gracious. In fact, in the very hour he was asked if he was the One, Jesus first healed many diseases, plagues, and handicaps before calmly answering John's question, affirming that he was the Messiah (Luke 7:21–23). He wasn't turned off by John's doubt, but instead used it to do more glorious work!

There are of course plenty of other examples to choose from (ahem, Doubting Thomas), but I wanted to start out by giving you just a taste of the real-life examples who went before you in biblical times and experienced true doubt. We'll look more closely at characters from Scripture in the following chapters, but for now it's important to understand that doubt is a normal part of Christian experience. Normal, like having someone stay over at your place.

We can see doubt as if it were like a sporadic visitor who should be a welcome guest in the home of our heart. Guests can come in and shake things up a bit in your home, but then they leave. Doubt should never take up permanent residence in your heart.

In addition to that, doubt can make us stronger. James 1:3 says that something like the hardship of our doubt produces steadfastness as our faith is tested. Yes, faithfulness can be grown in the soils of doubt. The Bible helps us see this and grants us the grace it takes for us to walk consistently with God through the ups and downs of our faith.

Reflection Questions

1. When you've struggled with doubt in the past, have you been prone to keep it to yourself or share what you're experiencing with others? What happened, as a result of your choice?

2. What would it specifically look like for you to engage with your doubts in an honest way, involving others you trust to help you through it?

3. Read James 1:3. In light of this text, along with the biblical examples we've looked at in this chapter, how do you think God

responds to us when we doubt? How is he currently working, and what is he producing in your life through your doubts?

CHAPTER TWO

Calm Down about Doubt

I don't think anyone who's ever met me would describe me as relaxed. Moderately to highly anxious? Yes. Relaxed? No. I'll never be the kind of person who saunters into a room with the kind of easygoing aura normally attributed to a southern California surfer dude who just drank thirty milliliters of cough syrup. I'm just not wired that way.

In fact, even as I write this, my left knee is bouncing up and down on the ball of my foot as it physically reacts to all the restless thoughts currently running through my brain. As much as I'd like to say this is an abnormal thing for me, unfortunately it's not. Consequently, when it comes to my doubts about God, I've never been able to have a calm or breezy attitude when it creeps into my life.

I can remember once, when a dating relationship of mine ended, thinking that God had no idea what he was doing. *Surely he's not sovereignly in control of my life because she was my perfect match!* I thought. *And if he's not in control of this, he's probably not in control of other things too. Ah! I'm freaking out!*

Now, maybe you're not a total spaz like me, but certainly at some point you've had somewhat irrational thoughts concerning God that snowballed into much grander dramatic conclusions that ran in stark contrast to the truth of Scripture. Big questions about God usually arise when our understanding or expectations of him don't line up nicely with our experiences. Practically every Christian I've ever known has been there at least once, and it can really unsettle and trouble us.

But what if, in those moments, we weren't worried or panicked? What if we trusted in the Lord and simply calmed down about our doubts? A life like that would drastically alter our day-to-day uncertainties.

Perhaps in the past, anxious, doubtful thoughts have left you sleepless, stressed, exhausted, or even angry. But have you ever stopped and asked what's at the heart of your anxiety? Why do we get worried when we doubt?

I'll admit that worry is often the default setting in my heart. I don't like it when I'm not in control. The unknown can be a great source of anguish for me, because I'm a control freak. I want everything to be under my rule and reign, so when my doubts raise up worry it's usually a good indicator that I want to place my faith more in myself than in the God of the universe. But a mistrust of God and full trust in myself is foolishness. Whenever I'm able to calm down and take a hard look at what's really going on in my heart when I'm worrying because of doubt, I'm able to see how ridiculous it is to freak out.

Do I really think I'm more capable than God? I have to sleep for a third of my life just to survive, and I get heartburn when the pasta sauce I've eaten has too much acidity in it! I'm nothing! I need to calm down—and perhaps you do too. When big questions come up, not panicking about our doubts is an act of faith in and of itself. So take comfort in the fact that God is God and you're not.

Two Options, Two Outcomes

When worry and anxious thoughts persist because of our constant dwelling on our doubts, it poisons the well of our spiritual lives. I'm not saying that you aren't a faithful Christian if you're experiencing anxious thoughts because of doubt. The struggle with anxiety can be a lifelong battle even for mature believers. What I am saying, though, is that there's a difference between experiencing anxiety and walking in it. Walking consists of steady, repeated actions one can keep up in a sustained way for a long period of time. Walking in anxiety eventually molds a person into someone who's characterized by anxiety. It becomes his or her identity, and identity is much different than a periodic struggle. I want to make sure we're on the same page here and have a healthy understanding of the difference between the two.

Anxiety and faith consistently battle it out in our hearts for the purpose of claiming ownership of our lives. One governs while the other does not. In fact, I'd be so bold to say that anxiety and faith cannot drive our hearts at the same time; and the Christian evangelist George Müller would agree with me: "The beginning of anxiety is the end of faith, and the beginning of true faith is the end of anxiety."[1] A life of anxiety cannot exist side by side with a life of faith. Faith and anxiety lead in two opposite directions. Let me break this down in three practical ways.

First, faith brings peace, and anxiety because of doubt brings turmoil. When I'm walking with God and trusting in his sovereignty over my life, I'm resting in him. My life is peaceful because I believe in his benevolent hand over every facet of my existence. However, if I'm constantly doubting whether or not God is who he says he is, if Jesus is the only way to heaven, or if the Bible is really true, the posture of my heart is one of worry and restlessness. I'm tortured by the millions of negative possibilities that could happen to me or the people I care about, and I dwell in a state of chaotic disharmony.

Second, faith amid doubt draws us closer to God, and anxiety because of doubt takes us from God. When I walk by faith, I'm making myself vulnerable for the sake of the gospel. This action is like working out a muscle—it gets progressively stronger with each use. And as my faith muscles get bigger I naturally draw closer to God, as I align myself with him and his purposes. All of a sudden, my doubt has produced strength in my relationship with God. Yet when I'm anxious as a result of my doubts, I'm distracted by my misgivings and concerns—to the point where my focus becomes all about my frustrating circumstances. My eyes drift to my pessimistic issues and away from my Savior.

Third, faith changes your life; anxiety because of our doubt changes nothing. As I exercise my faith muscles, God shapes and molds my heart into the likeness of his Son. I take steps of faith and become more and more like Jesus. I'm changed from the inside out and my life looks different from the old person I used to be (2 Corinthians 5:17). On the other hand, worrying about the issues my doubts have raised is tantamount to sitting in a rocking chair. I spend lots of time and energy rocking back and forth, but ultimately it'll get me nowhere. Anxiety because of doubt changes nothing.

The Endless Cycle

Again, I'm not a relaxed person—I'm more anxious. And when my doubts spawn anxiety in my heart, I become afraid. I'm fearful that God isn't really in control, isn't really kind or loving, doesn't have a plan for me—and that bad things are going to happen. It's this weird cyclical slog through negativity in my heart. I'm doubtful about whether or not God is in control of all things (sovereign), which makes me anxious, which leads to constant fear about the horrors of life, which makes me doubtful about his supremacy all over again.

See? It's this endless cycle of doubt, anxiety, and fear. It's sitting in the rocking chair, going back and forth, back and forth, back and forth—time, energy, and churning stomach acid—yet I'm getting absolutely nowhere.

But what if, instead of responding to doubt with anxiety, I took a more relaxed approach with my doubts when they inevitably arrived? What if, when gripped by anxiety, I focused not on my anxiousness but on the peace that only comes from trusting in God's power and love? Unquestionably, I'd worry a lot less and live with significantly more serenity in my heart. A life of peacefulness sounds nice—and believe it or not, it's actually possible even when we doubt.

Peace from the Typhoon

I grew up as a military brat, meaning my stepdad (whom I call my dad) was in the Air Force, and we moved frequently. I lived in a lot of interesting places, and when I was in late elementary school my dad got stationed at an airbase on the island of Guam. For two years, my family and I lived in the tropics. In case you've never heard of it, Guam is this little island way out in the Pacific Ocean near the Equator, about four thousand miles west of Hawaii. It's a place of tropical excitement and exhilarating adventure, but also an environment that is no stranger to typhoons—what I like to call a hurricane on crack.

And wouldn't you know it, during mid-January of our first year there, Typhoon Roy hit the island of Guam, and hit hard. All of our windows were boarded up, trees were blown over and uprooted, coconuts flew through the air and smashed into car windshields, rain fell at monsoon levels, and electricity was lost on the entire island for days.

Thinking back, I vividly remember the first night of chaos as Roy raged outside our little home on the airbase. I stood at the dining room table with my mom and sister and helped put together a thousand-piece jigsaw puzzle by candlelight as we listened to the destruction-producing storm howl outside. The average ten-year-old boy is brave when it comes to garden-variety adventure around the house, but I've got to admit that Typhoon Roy scared me half to death. Every creak, bump, and bang I heard outside made me jump with fear of what might happen if our storm shutters didn't hold up against the wind. Was God going to protect us during the storm? I doubted it.

My mom, sister, and I worked well as a team, but after about fifty pieces into the dimly lit puzzle my bladder got the best of me. I needed to go, which meant one more frightening thing: walking to the bathroom at the back of the house by myself in the darkness. So I manned up, grabbed the flashlight on the kitchen counter, and made my way to the back of the house.

When I reached the entrance to the hallway that led to our home's bedrooms and bathroom, I stopped short before continuing and noticed how dark the hallway appeared. In the dim flashlight illumination, our clothes hamper at the end of the hall looked remarkably like one of the tree goblins from my nightmares. I knew it was just my imagination, but what I heard next wasn't a creation of my mind. It was something quite real.

A strange hissing noise came from around my feet and startled me to the point of jumping backward, away from the hallway's entrance. Was it our lazy house cat, Muffin, looking for a back scratch or refill on her tiny bowl of cat food? I couldn't be sure, so I reluctantly let my flashlight beam fall to the ground near my feet, toward where the sound was coming from. Was I safe? I doubted it.

What I saw next changed my perspective on everything running through my mind that evening, and probably gave me the ability to recall this story with as much vivid detail as I can now. The narrow beam of light quickly revealed not Muffin the fat cat, but my sweaty dad in full workout gear, hissing while doing push-ups on the carpeted floor.

At this time in his life, my dad was a marathon runner, and if he wasn't able to get outside to exercise (like if there was a *typhoon destroying the island of Guam*, for example), he would work out at home by doing sit-ups, push-ups, and any stretching on the living room floor. I came across him while he was smack in the middle of his in-home workout.

As you can imagine, it was a little jarring for me in the moment, but when my flashlight lit up my dad as he made that exhaling push-up hissing noise, I remember feeling this immediate wave of peace that swept over my little mind and body. My doubts drained away, and I wasn't afraid of the dark hallway anymore. The sounds of the storm outside didn't scare me the way they did before. The clothes hamper at the end of the hall was just a piece of wicker furniture, not some scary monster.

There was my father, looking all manly and tough, and I took solace in the fact that he would protect me from any would-be dangers going on outside. He wouldn't let any creature that lurked in the darkness grab my legs and gobble me up. He would care for me and let no harm befall me. My doubts recoiled in the light of his protection and strength because I knew one thing for certain: my dad loved me.

As an adult now, I look back on this story as a wonderful example of how much God loves and cares for me. When I was a kid, I knew my dad would protect me from anything that tried to harm me, and my doubts that night were vanquished the second I saw him exercising on the floor. My dad is a great example of earthly love and protection, but God is infinitely more loving and caring than any earthly father could be. The evidence is here: "So if you sinful people know how to give good gifts to your children, how much more will your heavenly Father give good gifts to those that ask him" (Matthew 7:11, NLT).

Many of us constantly struggle with doubt and the resulting worry, anxiety, or paralyzing fear. Doubts about God. Doubts about God's control of the future. Doubts about God forgetting all about us or not loving us. Those suspicions can color our lives if we let them, but God calls us as his children to something much better than time-wasting worry. If we look to our heavenly Father and trust him when we doubt, our anxiety will melt like a crayon in the sun because we know he loves us (John 3:16–17) and wants what's best for us (John 10:10). It may not be immediately apparent, but we can always look to our Father as the way to alleviate the doubt-induced anxiety that has a nasty habit of sitting in the driver's seat of our lives.

Typhoon Roy brought not only destruction to Guam that year, but it also brought doubt and fear to the heart of a little boy who then quickly recognized that his dad was a safeguard in the storm. If we recognize that God is in fact God and that he is for us, not against us (Isaiah 43:1–5), worry because of our doubts will diminish in our lives and leave room for growth, faith, and intimacy with our Father. Our faith in his goodness guides us toward peace—a peace that rests in the relaxed confidence of his sovereignty when we're tempted to doubt it.

The antidote to the poison is clear. True peace comes from the source of life itself. In him we can rest and grow even stronger in our faith when doubt bubbles to the surface in our hearts. The more attention we pay to our doubts, the more attention they demand. So let's not worry when doubts show up; let's accept them as a natural part of our faith.

Big questions will inevitably come up in your walk with God, and have the ability to send us reeling in a cloud of worry. However, there are great and satisfying answers to your questions if you take the time to intentionally go after them, instead of staying on the sideline in a pit of anxiety. Remember the rocking chair that gets you nowhere, and instead lean strongly into your faith. God has met me there on multiple occasions when I've moved toward him and away from anxious doubt, and I bet he'll meet you there too.

Reflection Questions

1. What's at the heart of your anxiety when doubts arise? Take some time to process through what's genuinely going on in your core when you feel anxious because of doubt.

2. While anxiety can be a lifelong struggle for even a mature believer, in what ways has walking by faith reoriented your heart and brought peace, shifting your gaze away from looking at life in a negative way?

3. What would it practically look like for you to rest and grow stronger in the Lord when doubts inevitably come into your life? List some specifics.

CHAPTER THREE

Feed Your Faith, Not Your Doubts

Have you ever noticed that when you focus on one specific problem in your life, the normal things you deal with every day tend to fade into the background? For example, not too long ago, multiple warning lights on my car's dashboard popped on during a road trip I was taking with my wife and kids, including the dreaded "check engine" light. I couldn't think about anything else other than the fact that my car needed maintenance as soon as possible. It was difficult to focus on the subject matter my family was talking about throughout the rest of the day. I couldn't enjoy my lunch, or even be excited about my destination at the end of the trip. All I could think about were those warning lights.

You've probably experienced something like this before too—maybe not the exact car-related situation I just described, but surely someone or something has captured your attention with such strength that it has pushed nearly everything else in your life to the back burner. Human nature tends to obsess over negative or potentially negative thoughts and ideas in a way that's difficult to escape.

Doubt Scenario

Let me break down a doubt-related scenario for you that has occurred in my mind and heart a few times in the past. See if you can relate to this line of thought:

1. An article, blog, podcast, or video posted online makes a strong argument opposing the validity of Christianity.
2. I read or watch said post.
3. I can't retort in a way that can act as a logical counter to what I've seen or heard, because I don't know enough or haven't studied as much as the person who posted.
4. I begin to wonder if the argument they've posted can be answered in a satisfying way. I don't have the answer, so maybe nobody has the answer.
5. There's a tremor in the foundation of my Christian belief, and I begin to assume this argument against Christianity might be legitimate.
6. If this argument is accurate, maybe others against my faith are correct too.
7. I've based my belief system on something that might be false. I'm doubting the authenticity of Christianity.
8. If Christianity isn't true, maybe the Bible isn't either. Maybe God doesn't exist.
9. The world and everything in it explodes.

Okay, that last one is a bit of an exaggeration, but I think you get my point. I'm not saying this happens every time I've seen a well thought-out post online that's made me doubt, but perhaps this was (at least in part) something curiously similar to what you've experienced at some point in the past too.

The progression of thought here is important. Things start off relatively normal at the beginning (#1–3), but the more attention I pay to doubtful thoughts, the more they're nurtured by my mind and heart. As they're fed, they develop and expand into other, more illogical doubts and negative thoughts. The first thought domino falls, and I choose not to stop the subsequent tumbling downward to despair.

Feed your doubts and your faith will starve.[1] It's an almost inevitable outcome. As I mentioned in the introduction, it's similar to a child who constantly seeks the attention of his parents.

Doubt demands more and more of the spotlight the longer you linger on it, and it can easily transform into something ugly (like the world blowing up) if you allow it. When you allow your mind and heart to regularly become preoccupied by doubt, your faith gets neglected and becomes spiritually malnourished.

Think about This

Conversely, if you feed your faith, your doubts will starve.[2] So what is feeding your faith? Well, if you're intentional about dwelling on the beauty of God and his Word, doubt will have no room to fester in your heart and your faith will grow. Consider what the apostle Paul writes in his letter to the Philippians: "Finally, brothers, whatever is true, whatever is honorable, whatever is just, whatever is pure, whatever is lovely, whatever is commendable, if there is any excellence, if there is anything worthy of praise, think about these things" (Philippians 4:8).

When we actually think about these things, an inevitable coinciding action will follow—the seeds of God's peace will flood your life (4:9). When we actively dwell on Christ Jesus instead of our recurrent doubts, it produces a life that is in step with God—a relationship unlike anything else we've ever experienced.

A life that is in step with God is a life lived under the authority of his rule. It's a life that yields to the Holy Spirit and his instruction about what to do, what to say, how to live, how to think, and overall who to be.

When we become Christians and receive the gift of God's payment for our sin through the life, death, and resurrection of Jesus Christ, God the Holy Spirit (the third person of the Trinity) comes to live inside us. He dwells inside our bodies and gives us the power to live the Christian life.

Yielding to the Spirit and walking with God moment by moment is a lifestyle. It's learning to depend on the Holy Spirit for his abundant resources as a way of life. As we walk in the Spirit, we have the ability to live a life pleasing to God (Galatians 5:16, 25), along with the fact that we experience intimacy with him and all he has for us (Galatians 5:22–23).[3] By faith, we experience God's power through the Holy Spirit (Ephesians 3:16–17), giving us the ability to feed our faith instead of our doubts.

Obedient Feeding

Jesus once said, "I am the vine; you are the branches. Whoever abides in me and I in him, he it is that bears much fruit, for apart from me you can do nothing" (John 15:5). Not all things, not some things, not even a few things—apart from Jesus you can do *nothing.* He is the One who makes it possible, through the power of his Holy Spirit inside us, to live the Christian life and focus on our faith instead of our doubts. He is the One who makes it possible to walk with him on a moment-by-moment basis and rejoice in the relationship we have with him because of his sacrifice on the cross. He is the One in whom we abide—not only in our faith but also in our seasons of doubt.

Yes, we must trust in him in order to see this happen, but abiding isn't just about living a life of faith and remaining passive. Abiding is also a call to godly action. The chorus of the old hymn "Trust and Obey" gives us a good idea of what it means to feed your faith by abiding in God:

> Trust and obey,
> For there's no other way
> To be happy in Jesus
> But to trust and obey.[4]

Faith is the starting point (trust), but the obvious next step afterward is obedience. Both elements are like two wings on a plane; each must be present in order for flight to be possible. When we obey God, we aren't only displaying that our hearts belong to him, but we're providing tangible evidence to the fact that God's Word is the place from which we take our marching orders. Obedience to Scripture isn't a requirement for a relationship with God, but rather an indicator that we already have a relationship with God. We aren't saved through obedience, but instead bear the fruit that shows that the roots of our hearts are already anchored in salvation. Where there is continual fruit, there is also root.

When we feed our faith, we spend consistent time in the Bible because we long for God's Word; it's an act of obedience. When we feed our faith, we spend time praying, not as a box to check off but because we love being in communion with our Maker; it's an act of obedience. Good nourishment and health depends on your food source, so where does your soul go to eat?

Feeding your faith and not your doubts is all about relying on the power of the Holy Spirit, living in obedience to Scripture, and leaning on him whether things are amazing or horrible. If your doubts seem to be smothering you, go to him in both the good times and the bad, and ask the Holy Spirit to give you the power to feed your faith. Ask him to give you passion for devouring God's Word on a daily basis, because the Bible is the food that feeds and nourishes our souls.

By the power of his Spirit, don't obsess over your doubts so that they easily turn into insurmountable problems leading you into despondency. Instead, walk by the Spirit's power, trust that apart from Jesus we can do nothing, and live a life characterized by biblical obedience.

Reflection Questions

1. In the past, how have you allowed your heart and mind to become preoccupied with doubt? How has that affected your faith?

2. What does intimacy with God look like in your life, and how can yielding to the Holy Spirit lead to greater intimacy and connection with Jesus?

3. How would your daily routine be different if you practiced feeding your faith and not your doubts?

CHAPTER FOUR

Knowing Only *about* God Can Lead to Doubt

In my ministry, I've had a number of opportunities to write and speak on the subjects that most resonate with young people. One such topic is romantic relationships in the modern age. I've found that thousands of young people all over the nation have been curious to hear my perspective about dating and relationships, simply because of my "extreme perspective" on what a romantic relationship should look like in today's culture. I'm not afraid to push students out of their comfortable ideas on how a relationship should look because of the cultural norms involving things like smartphones, social media, and texting.

We're all aware that most of the initial stages of getting to know someone these days happens within the context of the digital world. Whether you meet in person and then look him or her up online, or if you meet online and then do some research (ahem—stalking), almost every young person wants more information about a romantic person of interest, and it's usually available to them at any time or place. The internet makes this a real option, and nearly everyone I've talked to takes advantage via social media and texting.

As a result, a false intimacy can come about rather quickly because of the stalking that takes place. In other words, people think if they know *about* someone, they actually know him or her. But this isn't true. Knowing a lot of things about someone isn't at all the same as knowing someone personally.

I always warn students about this, especially on the romantic front, because you can create an idealized image of someone by knowing a bunch of facts about them. Then, if you expect to click with them in person because you happen to like all the same things that they do, your unmet expectations can lead to significant disappointment once you discover the real person behind all the social media facts.

In order to truly get to know someone, you need to spend quality time with that person. Knowing their favorite bands and their opinions about cool coffee shops is fine and all, but relationships aren't meant to be studied from a distance and then antiseptically plugged into your life once you gather enough pleasing facts. There's an art to relationship that is meant to play out in the context of togetherness over time.

Knowledge Only versus Heart Relationship

If knowing about someone isn't the same as truly knowing someone (e.g., social media versus real life), then logically speaking knowing a ton *about* God isn't the same as actually *knowing* God. In other words, it's absolutely possible to have studied Scripture, church history, and theology, yet still not know God personally.

James 2:19 states, "You believe that God is one; you do well. Even the demons believe—and shudder!" Along with this verse, we can clearly see in Matthew 4:1–11 when the devil tempts Jesus that Satan is extremely familiar with Scripture. This tells us that demonic forces believe in God, the evil one and his minions know about him, and that they are thoroughly acquainted with the Bible. In other words, head smarts about God don't always equal heart relationship. But a deep heart relationship with God is one of the biggest buffers against doubt. Even if you don't know a lot of biblical truths and can't win an apologetics debate, a life-changing relationship with God is a solid foundation to stand on, and it won't be swayed because of a lack of debate skills.

For example, if you're someone who was raised in a home that regularly attended church, youth group, and other Christian activities growing up, you may know all the right answers to the discussion questions after a Bible study, but that doesn't at all mean you know God personally. Now, don't misunderstand me. You might be an authentic Christian in a personal relationship with God and still know all the answers—I'm not saying you aren't a believer in Christ. What I am saying, however, is that knowing all the right answers *in and of itself* doesn't mean you've received the gospel and been reconciled to God through the blood of his Son.

There are plenty of Bible teachers on this planet who aren't followers of Jesus Christ. Men and women throughout the world might have read the Bible cover to cover, and studied Christianity forward and backward, yet are still not personally acquainted with God the Father through the Son. Vast cognitive knowledge doesn't always amount to legitimate relationship; in fact, it can often lead to lingering doubt or make you vulnerable when doubt comes around.

And that's my point. As a result of this sobering truth, there are many people who know a great deal about God, but their lack of relationship with him has left the door wide open for doubt to cripple and destabilize a semblance of faith. When there is a lack of relationship (despite how much someone knows), doubt can often fill in the gaps, driving a wedge between that person and intimacy with God. Of course, that doesn't always happen, but often when it comes to simply acquiring facts about God, a person can't often see the forest for the trees. Someone can be overwhelmed by the details about God to the point where it has obscured his or her overall understanding of what it means to truly know him.

David's Doubt

Sometimes only knowing *about* God can be a path that leads directly to doubt, and eventual unbelief, because it simply isn't personal. Let me give you an example that's relatively close to me.

David is someone I've known for quite a long time and is dear to me. He was raised in a Christian family and when I met him, he would have called himself a follower of Christ. Now in his late twenties, David has walked away from the faith. By his own admission, David has read the entire Bible, attended more than a thousand church gatherings, participated in a dozen multi-day spiritual retreats, read at least fifty books discussing Christianity, listened to hundreds of Christian podcasts, prayed for hundreds of hours, spent entire days striking up conversations with strangers to introduce them to the gospel, lived with other Christians, spent countless hours informally discussing spiritual matters with friends and colleagues, led Bible studies, preached a few sermons, and even made significant life decisions based on Christian convictions. By all accounts that could be seen, David was a Christian.

But therein is the problem, I think—what *could* be seen. Even in David's mind, he was a believer—a true follower of Jesus Christ. But when David took a World Religions class his sophomore year of college, things began to unravel. His professor challenged David and spun his brain like a top as she guided her class through two-to-three-week chunks of seeing the world through the lens of an atheist, Hindu, Jew, and Muslim. The seeds of doubt were planted in David's mind.

In the following months and years, David fed his doubts on a steady diet of secular viewpoints and ideals, along with lots of time spent with non-Christian people. His faith started to deteriorate when he considered alternative answers to life's hard questions that seemed as equally plausible to him as Christianity. He started dating a girl who identified as agnostic, and stopped attending church altogether.

In the middle of this journey away from Christ, David and I had the opportunity to have a deep conversation about what he believed and where his beliefs were taking him. I asked him a lot of questions and took note of the fact that his mind-set leaned more on the side of nonbelief than belief. It seemed to me that David knew a lot *about* God from his years being raised in a Christian environment, but he now seemed to be speaking as if he were past that "silly phase" of Christian belief back from when he was a child and less enlightened to the world's reality. We talked for hours that day, and in the end I challenged him to look into the important topic of Christ himself.

"Is Jesus Christ dead, or is he alive?" I asked. "If he's dead and his decayed body can be found somewhere in the Middle East right now, Christianity is not true. But if he's alive, the dominos will fall from there, and while some things in this world will seem confusing to you, you'll always be able to come back to the fact that Jesus is not dead. Put all your chips on that and it's a safe bet." (More on this in Chapter 7.)

But my words fell on David's proverbial deaf ears. He didn't need to do any more research on Christianity because he felt like he already knew it. He didn't do any further reading to that end because his mind was already made up.

Today, I see David often and still consider myself close to him. He's a delightful personality, funny, caring, generous, and kind to everyone he crosses paths with. By almost all accounts, David is a wonderful person. I'm just overwhelmingly sad at the fact that he has all of those God-given qualities but no longer gives credit where credit is due. Kindness to him is an end in and of itself. Care and generosity are in the name of care and generosity instead of in the name of Jesus. For David, doubt became unbelief.

Now, I'm not going to take the time here to go into the theological arguments for and against whether or not David ever really was a Christian to begin with, because that's not my job to ascertain—it's God's. What I will say, however, is that I still have great hope for David, and I pray for him often. I pray that he'll have a genuine encounter with God and recognize that what he knew before as a young man was probably just knowledge in his head and really something that needed to travel 18 inches down to his heart. I pray that he wouldn't hold on to the attitude of "oh, I already know all about Christianity and I don't buy it," and have an authentic personal relationship with the living Christ.

Maybe you can see some similarities between David's life and your own, so this is probably a great time to ask you if you've truly come to a personal relationship with Christ. Have you? Do you know a ton *about* God or do you sincerely *know* him? As we've seen, the space between the head only and the authentic heart is eternally massive and worth the work of healthy introspection.

Don't Wither

Sometimes knowing isn't really knowing. There are many steps on the path (David's path took years), and many small choices are made along the way in order to arrive at unbelief. If you only know about God and don't really know God, you're in dangerous territory.

When you make intentional choices to move away from godly resources as you battle doubt, you're severing your link to the lifeblood of faith (John 15:1–6), and anything that's severed will wither. If a branch that bears fruit is cut off from the trunk of an apple tree, the apples will not thrive; they'll wither and die. Similarly, you must stay connected to God's Word, God's people, and God's Spirit because they are your spiritual resources. To proactively neglect them is to walk down the path toward unbelief. When doubt creeps in, don't let it steer you toward unbelief. Instead, learn to doubt in a healthy way—invest in your personal relationship with God through Jesus Christ, and let your doubts strengthen your faith instead of weaken it.

Reflection Questions

1. Why are the most important people in your life more than just people you know a lot of information about? How are your relationships with those people more significant?

2. Is there anything in David's story that you personally connect with? List any similarities you have with his doubt below.

3. Do you know a ton *about* God or do you sincerely *know* him? Take some time to pray through the answer to that question before God. Talk to him about where you currently stand and if you don't like what you see about your relationship with him, ask him to extend grace to you. Receive the payment Christ made for you, and be born again into the living hope (1 Peter 1:3). It is the greatest and most important decision you will ever make.

CHAPTER FIVE

Roads to Unbelief

In light of what we've been covering here, you might be wondering how doubt can grow and morph into unbelief. Perhaps you're finding yourself wrestling with doubt right now, and stories like David's frighten you about the possibility of ending up in the same place. If that's you, let me remind you of the truths we talked about in chapter 2, and encourage you to lean into the peace of a faith-filled life instead of the turmoil of a worry-filled one.

Now, let's explore a few specific roads that can end with abandoning the faith. Yes, there are several possible routes that unbelief can come from, but I want to cover only three here in this chapter, because I feel that these three[1] are probably the most common among young people.

1. Unrealistic Attitude

The first possible route I feel needs to be addressed for you, specifically as a young person, is the road that gets built through an unrealistic attitude in relation to faith. Theologian Alister McGrath argues, "If you believe you can, or need to, know everything with absolute certainty, your faith will be on rocky soil very soon."[2]

He's right. I have met and talked with many students and graduates who feel they have the right to know everything about the nature of God and how he works. There is so much dangerous pride in this mindset. When we discover that some facets of our faith are a mystery and have been so for thousands of years, in a lack of humility we can angrily jump to the conclusion that we have a right to know. Or in our arrogance, we believe we actually have the ability to understand everything. How pompous: if we don't possess the answers to difficult questions about God or the Bible, we simply assume there aren't any answers. Deep down, an attitude like this claims that we think we're equal to God in knowledge or understanding.

And as one doubt leads to another, we can become skeptical that belief in God and the Christian faith is illogical and somewhat silly. But just because we don't know everything about God doesn't mean we as human beings have the ability to uncover those obvious mysteries. Sure, there are plenty of things we can know and understand about God, but those things usually take time, study, and faith. At the end of the day, however, there will always be mysteries we will never completely understand because God is God—he is higher and profoundly different from us (Isaiah 55:8–9).

Our desire for answers can certainly be taken to the extreme, but it's important to remember that many skeptics and doubters have gone before you, and that the burning questions you're asking have been asked and smartly answered before; you just have to be willing to do the research in order to find them. But keep in mind God is under no obligation to prove himself to us—he already did that through the life, death, and resurrection of Jesus Christ, and if we're not ready to accept Christ as his final answer, we aren't ready to accept God at all (see Colossians 1:15–20).

Remember our two students, Ben and Kyle, who I mentioned at the beginning of this book? Near the end of our conversation that summer, I asked both of them how much research and reading they had done in order to get some solid answers to their important questions. At one point, I literally said, "What you're asking has been answered nicely by Tim Keller in his book *The Reason for God.*"

After I said that, Kyle asked, "Who's Tim Keller?"

I almost rolled my eyes. I wondered how in the world they didn't know who Keller was because of all the incredible resources he's created over the last few decades that directly address questions from skeptics. If those two guys wanted to doubt well, they seriously needed to do some reading. The answers to almost all their doubtful questions had already been satisfyingly answered by theologians, professors, authors, and pastors—they just needed to go find them.

And therein lies my point. How much authentic research have you done when seeds of doubt were planted in your mind? Have you really looked for the answers to your questions, or are your doubts possibly motivated by the arrogant position of an unrealistic attitude toward faith? If you put in the work, you'll be able to find some fantastic answers and explanations to your doubts, because your questions were someone else's questions a long time ago.

That said, however, faith isn't ultimately about absolute certainties. It's about a willingness to trust in the promises of God and the saving work of Christ, knowing that one day our trust will be vindicated.[3] One day we'll have all our questions answered; but for the moment, we walk by faith, not by sight.

Faith is never something in which we can be 100 percent sure—because there's no faith in that! Yet as you wrestle with doubts, there are innumerable answers to many of your questions if you're simply willing to look for them.

2. Morbid Preoccupation

Second, a road to unbelief can be constructed when and if we have a morbid preoccupation with doubt.[4] Sometimes our doubts tend to occupy every part of our thoughts and feelings, to the point that they can become obsessions. Then those obsessions can lead to a constant questioning about why we're obsessing in the first place. The doubts build and build until God himself is shut out.

There are many reasons why people obsess over or ruminate on their doubts. It can be oddly irresistible to perpetuate a cycle of negative and brooding thoughts, especially when something as important as God is the subject. Ultimately, though, as psychologist and counselor Elizabeth Scott explains, "it matters less *why* people obsess over [doubt], and more how they can stop."[5]

In response to negative obsessions, secular counselors or therapists usually recommend building better habits as a way of life, and putting those habits into practice when dark and obsessive thoughts creep up.[6] As followers of Christ, however, we know that the solution to life's problems cannot be found by looking inward toward ourselves in order to muster up the strength we need to tackle them. In fact, Jesus says it's just the opposite: "If anyone would come after me, let him deny himself and take up his cross and follow me. For whoever would save his life will lose it, but whoever loses his life for my sake will find it" (Matthew 16:24–25). Christ calls us as his followers to deny ourselves, take up our crosses (die to ourselves), and follow him. We needn't look inward to get rid of unhealthy obsession with doubt, but instead look outward toward him. Keeping in mind God's loving character, we are called to dwell on the promises in the Bible—to receive and savor them as God's very words. For example, Malachi 3:6 says, "For I the LORD do not change," and this promise is a soothing comfort in an unsteady culture that constantly shifts with the tide of public opinion. I love knowing how consistently dependable God is when my fickle heart doubts. And his promises in Scripture are everywhere:

> The love of the Lord never ceases, his mercies never come to an end. (Lamentations 3:22–23)
>
> He blots out our transgressions and does not remember our sin. (Isaiah 43:25)
>
> He is good, forgiving, and loving. (Psalm 86:5)
>
> He is near the brokenhearted and saves the crushed in spirit. (Psalm 34:18)
>
> He is slow to anger. (Exodus 34:6)
>
> He gives eternal life in Jesus Christ. (1 John 5:11–13)

He is eternal—the first and the last, the beginning and the end. (Revelation 22:13)

And on and on. The Bible is God's Word, and it's crucial that we dwell on the promises therein. If the eternal God who created everything decided that he wanted to personally communicate with me, I wouldn't put that off or neglect that message; I'd drink it in whenever I could. And guess what? That's the Bible! God's personal message.

Psalm 1:2 states that the righteous man delights "in the law of the LORD, and on his law he meditates day and night." Likewise, Joshua 1:8 says, "This Book of the Law shall not depart from your mouth, but you shall meditate on it day and night, so that you may be careful to do according to all that is written in it." From these verses and many more in Scripture, we can easily see that we should be meditating on the Word both day and night, not obsessing over our doubts.

Ask the Holy Spirit who lives inside of you if he would help your mind to stop allowing doubts to dominate your life. In the process of communing with God's Spirit and meditating on his Word, you'll rediscover the joy of faith and spiritually grow instead of shriveling.

3. Faith That Refuses to Grow Up

The third and final road I'll cover here is a path to unbelief that may come through an immature faith—a faith which refuses to grow up.[7] The process of maturing as followers of Christ involves deepening our understanding of what we believe. To neglect this process is to remain spiritual infants. And a baby can be a vulnerable, easily attacked, and possibly damaged by the doubts that lead to unbelief.

A weak faith is a defenseless faith. You are never meant to plateau in spiritual maturity as you walk with God. All of us as Christians are meant to grow deeper as we get older, leaving behind the things that bothered us when we were young in the faith.

Most of the doubts I had in my early years as a Christian came from an insufficient understanding of my faith. I asked questions and sought answers from the older and wiser believers I knew, read, and listened intently as the Bible was taught to me. I took the time to reinforce my faith with understanding, much in the same way a construction crew would reinforce concrete with steel. McGrath argues, "Together, [faith and understanding] can withstand far greater stress than they could ever withstand on their own."[8]

I became a Christian in the late 1990s. At that time, a little book entitled *More Than a Carpenter*[9] by Josh McDowell was a helpful tool that helped me proactively battle my doubts with relentless logic and clarity. It was the writing on subjects like security in my salvation, Jesus's historical identity as God's Son, and the Bible's reliability that reinforced my "concrete and steel" in a way that not only erased many of my doubts but directed me into a greater understanding of God—and thus, deeper, more meaningful worship.

How to Doubt Well

Doubt becomes unbelief when you *let* it become unbelief. When you cling to unrealistic ideas about the Christian faith, get hopelessly preoccupied with doubts that are a natural part of the life of a believer, or fail to allow your faith to grow, you are making active choices to move to unbelief.

It's important not to be ashamed of your doubts. When you are, hiding, isolation, and loneliness become the natural by-product. Consequently, the cycle of shame, hiding, isolation, and loneliness feeds on itself, driving you further away from your faith.

Instead, embrace the opportunity doubt gives you. Let it strengthen you in ways you could never have imagined. There are a few critical steps you can take to help you "doubt well" and grow stronger in your faith, as opposed to traveling down the roads to unbelief. Here are three I'd recommend.

1. Talk about your doubts with wiser Christians who will listen to you and walk with you in your difficulty. This can be a vital safety valve which stops a head of doubting steam from building up, eventually leading you from normal doubt to the hopelessness of unbelief.[10] I can't overstress how imperative it is to learn to doubt well by leaning into your questions within the environment of other believers. The Christian life is always meant to be experienced in the context of community and fellowship with other believers. When we begin to separate ourselves or break away from the pack, so to speak, a number of bad consequences start to creep into our lives. Our three enemies—the world, the sinful nature or "flesh," and the devil—can easily gain a foothold and influence our decision-making in a negative way. However, if we proactively involve other caring believers in our lives, they are often able to spot areas where we might be prone to compromise and succumb to the temptation that God is not present or that he doesn't care, leading directly to unbelief.[11]

If you want your relationship with God to be healthy and flourish on every level, you can't doubt in a vacuum, devoid of others. You need godly people in your life to give you balance and perspective, especially when you doubt. You need input from friends and family who are wiser than you. A Christian in isolation is a Christian in danger. Surround yourself with godly men and women who care about you and care about Jesus. When you do, you'll be laying the right kind of building blocks to your foundation, bringing honor to the Lord even as you wrestle with doubt.

2. Practice the habit of good orthodox reading—both books and online. One of the biggest regrets I have from my college years is that I didn't read enough. As a student, you're bombarded with crazy amounts of reading for your classes, and that can sour your desire for any additional reading while in school and even after graduation. Nonetheless, I encourage you to carve out intentional time every week to read and study writings that bolster your Christian faith.

Of course you need consistent, daily time in God's Word; but in addition to that, it's important to have a steady stream of theology, exhortation, and godly input in your life from writers old and new. Authors who have been instrumental to my Christian growth include C. S. Lewis, Tim Keller, Paul Tripp, Bill Bright,

John Piper, Jen Wilken, David Platt, A. W. Tozer, Charles Spurgeon, R. C. Sproul, Sam Allberry, Jackie Hill Perry, and Elisabeth Elliot. There is also an overabundance of fabulous content on sites like The Gospel Coalition and Desiring God.[12]

Read often and well in order to gain good perspective on your faith, and to learn satisfying answers to tough questions. I've never once wished that I had read less when I was younger. Don't use the excuse of being young, with your whole life ahead of you, to justify your lack of time in the written word.

3. Be a committed member—and regular attender—of a local church. If you're part of a community of believers with whom you are vulnerable, self-sacrificing, and accountable to godly living, you'll never doubt in isolation.

Watch any nature show and you'll quickly learn that predators set their sights on prey that isn't a part of the pack. It's easier to successfully attack when the prey is all alone with no one around to offer help or protection. We can learn from this example. There is a great deal of relational health in godly community, providing those who doubt with guidance, love, counsel, empathy, and grace.

As you navigate your faith, doubting well and avoiding the roads to unbelief require a great deal of intentionality. Many of us have a hopeful longing for God's peace when wrestling with doubt, but peace doesn't necessarily mean the absence of challenge. The roads to unbelief are clearly marked in the life of a young person, so let's be deliberate about where we're walking and anticipate that the temptations to stray will be prevalent in every stage of life.

The beginning of Hebrews 12:2 calls believers to fix our eyes on Jesus. If your eyes are fixed on something, your attention never moves from it. Much like the story of Peter walking on the water in Matthew 14, we must remain focused. When Peter walked on the water, he was looking at Jesus; his eyes were fixed on him. The moment Peter got into trouble and started to sink was when he became distracted by the wind and the waves, letting his gaze wander away from Christ. The wind and waves of doubt can be intimidatingly powerful in your life. Let's continue to look to

Jesus for comfort, power, and peace, even as the storm of doubt rages around us.

Reflection Questions

1. In what ways have you had an unrealistic attitude about knowing everything concerning the Christian faith? How has that attitude left you disappointed?

2. Instead of obsessing over your doubts, what specific Scripture verses can you meditate on that communicate God's promises?

3. Look again at the three recommended points above to help you doubt well. What is your specific plan of action to live in community, read widely, and commit to a body of believers?

CHAPTER SIX

Counting the Cost

We understand that dwelling on doubt for too long can lead to dark and dangerous places. Unbelief is a product of obsession over doubts, and my guess is if you're reading this book, that's a product you'd rather not pursue. Why? Because the cost of belief is high, but the cost of unbelief is infinitely higher. Let me explain what I mean.

It can be quite difficult to be a Bible-believing follower of Christ as a young person in our present culture. To stand on the gospel and proclaim you believe Jesus is the Son of God, lived a sinless life, was slaughtered for the sins of humanity, rose from the dead, and that we must believe in him to be made right with God is regularly viewed as narrow, judgmental, and even bigoted by many in today's society. I've heard of and personally experienced mockery, marginalization, and even mild persecution because of faith in Christianity. Consequently, there's a very real cost to believing and following Christ. But conversely, when it comes to unbelief the cost skyrockets.

Although it might seem like there is tremendous freedom in not being tethered to belief in the true biblical God, the aftermath is actually quite depressing once you think about it. I'm reminded here of actor Jim Carrey's tongue-in-cheek speech at the 2016 Golden Globe Awards. Introduced as "two-time Golden Globe

Award-winning actor Jim Carrey," he then proceeded to humorously talk about true meaning, much to the laughter of the other Hollywood actors in the room. As he came to the microphone, here's what he said, through an intentional plastic smile:

> I am two-time Golden Globe winner, Jim Carrey. You know, when I go to sleep at night, I'm not just a guy going to sleep. I'm "two-time Golden Globe winner Jim Carrey" going to get some well-needed shut-eye. And when I dream, I don't dream just any old dream . . . I dream about being "three-time Golden Globe actor Jim Carrey"—because then I would be enough. It would finally be true, and I could stop this terrible search for what I ultimately know won't fulfill me.[1]

Clever, of course, but also bitingly true. Fulfillment in life ultimately can't be found in anything outside of God. And to live life in pursuit of the meaning only a relationship with God can provide is one continual disappointment. Even the rich and famous know this, because the "mountaintops" they conquer are deficient and shallow. Once God is ignored (agnosticism) or removed (atheism) from the narrative of a person's life, there will always be a cavity in that person. He or she will ache for a relationship with him while searching for contentment in never-satisfying fake substitutes.

Atheism, for example, has not yielded societies of more harmony and peace, but less. In fact, oppression is typically the result of unbelief. Alister McGrath says in his history of atheism: "The 20th century gave rise to one of the greatest and most distressing paradoxes of human history: that the greatest intolerance and violence of that century were practiced by those who believed that religion caused intolerance and violence."[2] This is the regular result of unbelief. I'm sure there are plenty of skeptics or atheists who would rather ignore this historical truth than cling to it because of its messiness, but it's there nonetheless.

Not only that, but unbelief gives a person no legitimate ground to stand on when it comes to moral absolutes. One might say they don't believe in God, but the way they live often proves otherwise. For example, almost any unbelieving young person would say that there are people in the world right now doing things they believe those people should stop doing, no matter what those people personally believe about the correctness of their behavior (e.g., rape, murder, injustice). But as Tim Keller points out rather cleverly: "Doesn't that mean that [one] *does* believe there is some kind of moral reality that is 'there' that is not defined by us, that must be abided by regardless of what a person feels or thinks?" The common response to his question (as noted in his book *The Reason for God*) is silence, either a thoughtful or a grumpy one.[3]

In other words, unbelief—true unbelief—produces absolutely no reason for moral standards. If there is no God to create a clearly defined set of absolutes about what is right or wrong, then murder, injustice, thievery, and violence shouldn't really mean anything at all. It can't be wrong if the definition of right and wrong is relative. Yet most people who claim a position of unbelief don't actually live that way. Why? Because if you really did live as if there were no set of moral standards, you'd be a monster. You wouldn't care about the value of human life, the way you treated people wouldn't matter, and if anyone ever harmed you it wouldn't be consistent of you to tell them they were wrong in doing so. Who's to say it's wrong if there's no God?

See, the popularly held secular position of unbelief is devastating once you follow it to its logical conclusion. What unbelief advertises as freedom is in reality horrid because it's anarchy. If you get to the belief behind the unbelief, however, most young people actually just want to do whatever they want to do without the gloominess of guilt hanging over their heads because of poor and selfish life choices. In my experience with the average secular young person, unbelief is really just an excuse for intellectual laziness. Where's the integrity in that?

Life with Meaning

Sure, belief has its costs. And depending on where you live, the cost could be your very life. Following Jesus in the Western world today, however, will more likely look like unfair prejudice and marginalization. But a life with meaning is certainly worth the cost, even if means becoming more uncomfortable in our increasingly secular culture.

A life without God (and therefore, meaning) might grant someone the "ease" of trying to find her own meaning and be her own god for a time, but the sense of purpose achieved isn't real purpose—it's hollow. Why? Because human beings were made for God.

If an auto mechanic builds a car that's designed to win any stock car racing event, that car is never going to plow a field of corn. It was built for a purpose and cannot reach its full potential in anything besides stock car racing. Similarly, if you're designed to live life in relationship with God but continually search for relationship with anything else, that thing will fail you—because whatever your "anything else" happens to be is not God.

Perhaps as a Christ-follower you won't experience the difficult costs of believing until later in life, but those costs are for a God-ordained purpose. When we believe in the biblical view of God and his loving sovereignty over our lives, we can see that life does have meaning.

At its heart, unbelief generates a life without meaning—a life that claims freedom, yet produces despair. As we consider this, the price paid for unbelief is far greater, and we must all count the cost. When we linger in the company of doubt, it can often lead to unbelief. Be careful about how you process and wrestle with your doubts. Look at the practical implications of your belief or unbelief. Think, pray, read your Bible, and seek godly wisdom from the people in your life who you trust to steer you in the right direction.

God will meet you in your doubts if you choose to seek him. In fact, Scripture tells us you'll find him in your pursuit. Proverbs 8:17 says, "I love those who love me, and those who seek me diligently find me."

Ask the Lord for help as you doubt. Reject the intellectual laziness of unbelief. He will meet you as you count the cost and settle on the fact that unbelief is simply foolishness.

Reflection Questions

1. Where have you searched for fulfillment apart from God? How have those substitutes failed you?

2. If any person's moral standards ultimately come from God, why do you think people try to live lives of unbelief built on moral standards?

3. How are the costs of belief for you small in comparison to the costs of unbelief?

CHAPTER SEVEN

It All Hinges on This

In all my time working with college students, the two most common doubts that spring to the top of the list for young people are 1) the Bible's validity or reliability, and 2) Jesus's resurrection from the dead. Let's take a closer look at each.

Trusting in God's Word

Before we address the resurrection, I think it's a good thing to take a little time exploring some of the facts surrounding the Scriptures, which can help us know that the Bible is a reliable foundation on which to build our lives.

The Bible is God's holy, inspired Word. It is the most powerful and quoted book in the world, and is responsible for changing not only my life but hundreds of millions of people's lives all over the world. The cofounder of Cru, Dr. Bill Bright, describes God's Word this way:

> The composition of the Bible is indeed amazing. A library of sixty-six books, it was written by more than forty different human authors under the divine inspiration of the Holy Spirit. These writers wrote independently, knowing almost nothing of the other's part. None had anything in common, and their literary qualifications were diverse. Moses, for example, was a man of learning, trained in the

> best universities of Egypt. Peter, on the other hand, was a fisherman without claim to formal education. Yet, each wrote the wisdom of God with powerful force. It took the Old and New Testament writers fifteen centuries to complete the Bible, which was written in three languages (Hebrew, Aramaic, and Greek) and on three continents. Indeed, this collection of books is really one, not sixty-six, for it is coherent in content and progressive in truth. The Bible is composed of 1189 chapters (929 in the Old Testament and 260 in the New) and utilizes 773,746 words to convey its life-changing message. This literary masterpiece contains history, laws, poetry, prophecy, biography, dramatic stories, letters, and revelations.[1]

It's incredible, really. Once you begin to think about Scripture's historical reliability, it starts to become clear that this collection of books is no mere collection. Only a little bit of research will lead you to conclude that the Bible is sound in its authenticity, and consequently the perfect foundation to build your life on.[2] And what is the cornerstone of that foundation? Jesus Christ.

Jesus is the Bible's central figure. His birth as the Jewish Messiah and Savior of the world was prophesied by Old Testament authors, and their writings contain more than 300 separate references to the coming of Jesus, including many with specific and unique details.[3] Christ fulfilled 100 percent of all the Old Testament predictions of the birth, life, death, and resurrection of the Messiah, written hundreds of years before Jesus was even born. He is what the Bible is all about. Once our hearts take hold of this fact, we can use our faith in him as a weapon against doubt.

This leads nicely into the other foundational doubt I've found to be most common among young people: whether or not Jesus really rose from the dead.

Are His Bones in the Ground?

Here's the center of Christianity: The resurrection of Jesus is the single most important event in history, because it acts as the hinge on which everything else in our faith swings. If Jesus Christ is dead, the Christian faith isn't true; but if he's alive, it has to be true. Tim Keller puts it this way: "If Jesus rose from the dead, then you have to accept all he said; if he didn't rise from the dead, then why worry about any of what he said? The issue on which everything hangs . . . is whether or not he rose from the dead."[4]

Why is this so important? That's an imperative question, and one I've asked before with sincerity. Perhaps you're like I was, and you genuinely want to know why what we celebrate on Easter is such a big deal. Proof of the resurrection itself can lead to the alleviation of doubt in your life.

There is substantial evidence for the resurrection of Christ. Professor Thomas Arnold (1795–1842) was the author of the famous three-volume *History of Rome* and chair of modern history at Oxford. He was well acquainted with the value of evidence in determining historical facts when he wrote, "I have been used for many years to study the histories of other times, and to examine and weigh the evidence of those who have written about them, and I know of no one fact in the history of mankind which is proved by better and fuller evidence of every sort, to the understanding of a fair inquirer, than the great sign which God has given us that Christ died and rose again from the dead."[5] Or another way to put it by Christian philosopher William Lane Craig: "When you . . . [use] the ordinary canons of historical assessment, the best explanation for the facts is that God raised Jesus from the dead."[6] So, what are the facts?

At the tomb after the resurrection, several truths were discovered. To start, the Roman seal was broken, which meant automatic crucifixion upside down for whoever broke it. The massive stone was moved not just from the entrance but from the entire sepulcher, looking as if it had been picked up and carried away.[7] The guard unit had fled. Byzantine Roman emperor Justinian, in his *Digest* 49:16, lists eighteen offenses for which a Roman guard unit could be put to death—including falling asleep or leaving one's position unguarded.[8]

The women came as the first ones on the scene, found the tomb empty, and then spoke to the risen Jesus. Keller explains why this fact is significant:

> The accounts of the resurrection in the Bible were too problematic to be fabrications. Each gospel states that the first eyewitnesses to the resurrection were women. Women's low social status meant that their testimony was not admissible evidence in court. There is no possible advantage to the church to recount that all the first witnesses were women. It could only have undermined the credibility of the testimony. The only possible explanation for why women were depicted as meeting Jesus first is if they really had.[9]

After that, 1 Corinthians 15:6 tells us that Jesus then appeared to more than five hundred brothers at the same time, most of whom were still living when the apostle Paul wrote 1 Corinthians. The empty tomb combined with the eyewitness accounts makes the resurrection even more historically certain. New Testament scholar N. T. Wright argues, "If there had been only an empty tomb and no sightings, no one would have concluded it was a resurrection. They would have assumed that the body had been stolen. Yet if there had been only eyewitness sightings of Jesus and no empty tomb, no one would have concluded it was a resurrection, because people's accounts of seeing departed loved ones happen all the time. Only if the two factors were both true together would anyone have concluded that Jesus was raised from the dead."[10]

Paul's letters tell us that Christians proclaimed Jesus's bodily resurrection from the very beginning, and this meant the tomb must have been empty. Why? As Keller points out, "No one in Jerusalem would have believed the preaching for a minute if the tomb was not empty. Skeptics could have easily produced Jesus's rotted corpse. . . . [W]hatever else happened, the tomb of Jesus must have really been empty and hundreds of witnesses must have claimed that they saw him bodily raised."[11]

This is noteworthy, because in the first century there were many other messianic movements whose would-be messiahs were executed. However, as Wright points out, "In not one single case do we hear the slightest mention of the disappointed followers claiming that their hero had been raised from the dead. They knew better. Resurrection was not a private event. Jewish revolutionaries whose leader had been executed by the authorities, and who managed to escape arrest themselves, had two options: give up the revolution, or find another leader. Claiming that the original leader was alive again was simply not an option. Unless, of course, he was."[12]

There were tons of other messianic phonies whose lives ended the same way Jesus's did. Why would the disciples of Jesus have come to the conclusion that his crucifixion hadn't been a defeat but a triumph—unless they had seen him risen from the dead?[13]

Hopefully, this small window into the evidence of Christ's resurrection has whetted your appetite to dig in further. As you read some of the resources I've quoted from and others, you'll discover that substantial research has been done to account for the historical truth that Jesus's bones are not in the ground—he's alive.

The Central Point

The resurrection acts as the central point on which every other apologetic is built, and the main one you should focus on as you consider your doubts. If Jesus is alive right now and the resurrection actually happened, then he is who he said he was. There are multiple places in Scripture where Jesus talked about his resurrection from the dead, so we can understand with clarity that he knew he was going to be killed and after three days, come to life again.[14]

So, if Christ is risen from the dead, it also means that before he died he knew he would conquer death. This means he holds the keys to life and death itself. He is the Messiah, the Son of God, the King of kings, and Lord of lords—he was who he claimed to be

(John 8:58; 14:6–7). Naturally, then, everything he said while he was here on earth was true. And if everything he said was true, we also know that people he talked about from the Old Testament—such as Moses, Abraham, and Jonah—were actually real, which validates the entirety of Scripture, which says that God created the world and everything in it.

Do you see the progression of logic? Again, the resurrection is the hinge on which the door of our faith swings. There may be many problems in your personal heart and mind that cause you to doubt and question the validity of God, his Word, the Christian faith in general, creationism, eternity, or the existence of heaven and hell, and so on. But if Jesus is alive, those other doubts you're wrestling with will start to fade in the light of Christ's victory over death. Sure, there may be certain things about God you still don't understand or can't wrap your mind around, but you can always come back to the fact that Jesus is alive.

I remember the resurrection question being answered for me, and the subsequent peace I felt after discovering the historicity of Jesus Christ's resurrection. All the other doubts and questions I had were, of course, still worth exploring and working out over time, but I knew then that there would probably be things I would never figure out about the Lord in my lifetime. That was okay, however, because I was able to rest comfortably on the truth of the resurrection. There was a calmness to my mind and heart unlike anything I'd ever experienced. I may not have understood, or even now understand, the problem of evil, for example, but the resurrection points me firmly to the truth of God's love for people—and all of a sudden I am at peace. Not with evil, of course, but in knowing that God is God and I am not. My attempts to box him into my logical framework of how I think things ought to go are ridiculous.

Jesus is alive, and that fact alone covers over all of my doubts.

Look into It

I'm not trying to provide you with cold comfort here, pretending that I understand you and everything you may have suffered or personally gone through over the years that could cause your doubt. That would be insensitive of me. So when I say that if you're wrestling with doubts you should start by looking first at Christ's resurrection, I mean it as a caring exhortation from an older brother in Christ who was once where you are now.

I challenge you to start at the resurrection, because I genuinely believe it'll help your doubt. Do the research, and not just in the Bible; look into the historical evidence for the resurrection of Christ. I'm confident that if you do enough digging, you'll see that Jesus of Nazareth is in fact not dead, but alive.

Therefore, it's wise of me to give you a push in the direction of what I believe is the single most convincing argument for the existence of the biblical God we read about in Scripture—the resurrection of Jesus Christ from the dead. Discovering the truth that he is alive will hopefully lead you away from dark doubt and into the loving arms of God the Father, made known to us by God the Son, Jesus Christ, who equips us with power from God the Holy Spirit to live the Christian life, and bring glory to his name.

Reflection Questions

1. In what ways have you leaned into the doubt you might have—about the Bible, the resurrection of Jesus Christ from the dead, or the Christian faith—by doing the work of researching and finding answers?

2. Why is the resurrection the single most important event in history, and why is it the hinge of your Christian faith? Jot down your answers.

3. If Jesus is alive right now, how does that directly influence the doubts you might be wrestling with?

SECTION TWO

EVERYDAY DOUBTS

This section will help you walk through the inevitability of common doubts a Christian can experience each day, yet ones that essentially don't call into question the foundations of your faith. Don't get me wrong: everyday doubts can be quite dangerous if we aren't careful and let them fester over time in our hearts. *That's* why this section is so important—these doubts might not rock your faith to the core, but they have the ability to wear you down and erode your faith over time. Let's address them with courage and intentionality, then, so that we might doubt less.

CHAPTER EIGHT

Your Questions Are Important

One of the things I've loved about working with college students is that the university itself is an environment which encourages deep thought, intentional study, and a hunger for seeking answers. In short, college is usually a safe place to ask questions.

Typically, this happens all the time in the classroom, and rightly so. But a trend I've noticed among Christian college students is a reluctance to voice questions and confusion when it comes to seeking answers about God and related spiritual topics. There seems to be a bit of fear related to asking difficult questions in a way that outs the person asking. In other words, people are afraid that their questions will directly imply spiritual immaturity or a lack of faith. *I can't ask that question about God*, one might think, *because all of my Christian friends will then know that I'm doubting him, and they'll think I'm ditching my faith.*

Maybe you wouldn't think something like that, but there certainly exists a common anxiety within Christendom regarding vulnerably asking questions related to your struggles. I know this because I've talked to multiple young people over the years who've admitted it to me. There's an unhealthy fear of what others might assume about you if you speak up, so that fear generally leaves you to deal with your doubts in isolation . . . and as we've already discussed, isolation is never good.

And there's another reason students don't talk about their doubts, as John 12:42–43 describes: "Nevertheless, many even of the authorities believed in him, but for fear of the Pharisees they did not confess it, so that they would not be put out of the synagogue; *for they loved the glory that comes from man more than the glory that comes from God*" (emphasis added). Let me confess: The praise that comes from people is a sinful stumbling block I regularly pursue. Perhaps you're like me when I admit that I genuinely like it when others like me. It feels amazing when praise from other people washes over me.

And of course, the other side of that glory-that-comes-from-man coin is the fact that I hate being mocked or disdained. It can feel nearly impossible when I know I need to move toward something that will most likely generate scorn from other people—especially people I'm close with. Consequently, if I know that eyebrows will raise if I ask the kind of question that seems to indicate I'm wrestling with doubt, it's going to be terribly difficult to open my mouth and ask. Can you relate?

A Safe Place to Ask

I've met and talked with numerous young people who have had difficult questions but were unwilling to ask them publicly, for fear that their friends would think they weren't "good Christians." They saw their questions and doubts as signs of weakness or immaturity so they dealt with them privately, only serving to make their doubts fester and increase in strength.

But there should be no statute of limitations on your questions.[1] Just because you may have been a believer for a long time doesn't mean you can't ask questions anymore. The body of Christian community, if anywhere, should be the place where questions are welcomed. The church should invite sincere questions from men and women who are wrestling with doubt—not only so we can point them to resources and pray for them, but also so we can be godly friends to them and encourage them as they doubt. All of us need Christlike friends to lean on when the storms of life shake us up.

Additionally, we needn't be afraid of the questions themselves. Christianity has existed for nearly two thousand years, and has never collapsed in on itself because of inquisitive questions.[2] There should be a free and vulnerable environment among the Christians on your campus, in your church, with your believing friends, in your neighborhood, or in your campus ministry. Those are the places where nonbelieving people should feel safe to be skeptics, and in turn see the love of Christ shine brighter than anything they've ever seen before. If nonbelievers in your circle of influence continue to experience the kind of setting I just described amid your Christian community, you should get ready—because you're probably going to see lives transformed and people coming to Christ on a regular basis.

Questions aren't only important right now; they also prime the pump for creating healthy dialogue concerning the doubts that will inevitably come up as you get older. As a young person, you probably haven't experienced the "heaviness" of life just yet. You probably haven't experienced intense marital strife, had a miscarriage in the middle of trying to start a family, or seen one of your children walk away from the faith. Life can be incredibly difficult as you go through it, and when that difficulty arises, you will naturally begin to ask questions about God in ways you simply haven't before.

And that's okay. A Christian—young or old, immature or mature—should never feel like he or she should be above asking authentic questions that plague the heart. In his book *A Severe Mercy*, Sheldon Vanauken said after the untimely death of his wife, "To believe with certainty, one has to begin by doubting."[3] Strength often comes through questions and doubts, not weakness. In truth, someone who asks questions and brings their doubts to God may have a stronger walk with him than someone who just knows all the right answers during Bible study.

Jesus said this about children: "Truly, I say to you, unless you turn and become like children, you will never enter the kingdom of heaven. Whoever humbles himself like this child is the greatest in the kingdom of heaven" (Matthew 18:3–4). I always took these verses to mean that a childlike faith was a dumbed-down faith, a naïve faith. And while that may be true to a certain degree, I had two kids who started growing up and asking questions every waking moment of every single day. Children live in a constant state of wonder and curiosity about their environment and experiences. Like a sponge, they soak up as much information and knowledge they can as they develop personalities and start to make sense of the world—so they ask a lot of questions. A childlike faith isn't a dumbed-down faith; it's a question-asking foundation of faith that leads to answers, while producing joy in the journey.

Enter into the Joy

There is joy when we're on an adventure to find something we value. For example, when I was around eleven years old, my sister and I found what we believed to be a treasure map in the woods behind a friend's house. At first, we were skeptical of its authenticity because, you know, it was a treasure map—and to the best of our knowledge, pirates didn't bury chests of gold on landlocked Air Force bases like the one where we lived. But once we got our bearings and saw that the map in fact charted the geographic area of the very place where we were standing, we didn't care if it was real or not—we were going to follow that thing to its conclusion.

And so we did. About sixty jubilant minutes after my sister and I found the map, we were digging with our hands in the ground where the corresponding X was marked on that piece of paper. About two feet down into the dirt, we came across a small wooden box, no bigger than a high school Algebra textbook. I'll never forget the excitement I felt when we discovered that box. My sister literally squealed with delight, while my heart raced behind my little ribcage.

We plucked the mystery box from the earth, set it on the ground next to the hole where it was buried, and slowly opened up the lid on its top. We had no idea what would be inside, but the hysteria of that moment was no doubt the reason I can remember this story with such vivid detail nearly thirty years after it happened. Inside, the purple, velvet-lined box boasted two gold coins, one gold ring, and one thin gold chain.

My sister and I looked at each other in amazement. We couldn't believe that we had actually found buried treasure in the woods near our friend's backyard on a military base. We sprinted home, riches in hand, and nearly screamed the entire time we recounted the story to our parents—who, by the way, still claim to this day that they had nothing to do with the map or the treasure.

Sometimes as we seek God, he can seem difficult to find. And in the pursuit, it can be easy to doubt that he's there at all. But God's hiddenness is ultimately an invitation to look for him, not the opposite. One scholar's comment on the matter is something I find helpful when I feel God is missing: "When God seems to be absent, it is in no way a stiff-arm from the ethereal realm, but rather a request to enter into the joy of searching after him."[4]

Much like my treasure hunt when I was a kid, our search for God when he seems hidden can be a delightful experience, depending on our perspective in the process. When God appears to be veiled from our senses, he wants us to find him; and when we search, there can be great joy in the hunt. The questions you have about God imply interest in him and his methods, so pursue him as you ask and doubt. There just might be buried treasure in your future.

Longhorn Cows and Chronic Pain

I once took a trip to Austin, Texas, and was met by the most quintessential Texan thing upon leaving the Austin airport.

A friend and I rented a car at the airport, and as we pulled out of the parking deck to head for the highway, we realized that we had pulled in toward a dead end that stopped at a Texas Longhorn cattle ranch. We got out, and as I carefully tiptoed up to the fence enclosure, multiple longhorn steers trotted to me. Their horns were fascinating, some jutting straight out away from the cow's head and then spiking upward toward the sky, some twirling outward like partially unraveled corkscrews probably measuring nearly seven feet from point to point. In all my years, I had never seen cows like these. I was in awe of how huge their horns were.

One longhorn in particular had a brownish-orange coloring, mixed with white splotches. But his coloring wasn't what made me focus on this guy—it was the size and shape of his horns. This steer was unique among his peers, as he was probably much older than the rest of the herd. His head hung low to the ground and bobbed left to right as he walked slowly in front of me, undoubtedly burdened by the weight of the massive horns that twisted outward from his head. From tip to tip, I guessed that the width of those horns most likely outmeasured the length of our rental car, and they clanked hard against the cattle guard in the ground as he moved.

A solitary thought repeated in my brain over and over as I watched this beautiful creature, as if God was trying to remind me of something in the moment: this cow's burden is the very thing that makes him special. His heavy and awkwardly shaped horns are his hardship, but they're also what makes someone like me marvel at how beautiful he is.

I thought about that for weeks. Eventually I asked a friend of mine who's a Texas native about the animals and why they can't have their horns removed to ease their burden. My friend said that if you cut off the horns of these cows, water from the rain will seep into the stumps; it will begin to rot the remainder of the horns, causing an infection and eventually death—or water will seep into their sinuses and they'll drown. The horns have to stay so the cow can survive; they're a lifelong load that the animal has to carry.

As mentioned earlier, I've wrestled with chronic pain. For ten years, it's been a trial for me due to a bulging disc in my spine that pushes on my sciatic nerve and makes my leg throb and ache on an almost consistent daily basis. I've tried nearly everything to eliminate the problem, even seeing the top neurosurgeon at Penn Medicine who said if I had surgery, I might come away with even more pain.

Needless to say, it's been easy for me to doubt God through all of this, and I don't think many would blame me for doing so. But as I've doubted, I've learned much and asked God many questions. My chronic struggle, much like our set of cow horns, has certainly become the heavy burden I carry with me wherever I go. It's the reason my "head can hang low," so to speak, and make my outlook on life sometimes feel cumbersome and sullen.

Yet simultaneously, my pain has been the vehicle by which God has shaped me and molded me into the man I am today. In the last decade or so, as I've doubted and asked numerous questions of God, my physical pain has been the primary way by which I've been able to identify with Christ and his sufferings. I've learned to a tiny degree that my Savior was in misery when he was beaten and crucified as God the Father turned his face away from his Son. His life was constant hardship—and he went through all of that for *me*.

My experience with pain has been visceral in a way that nothing else in my life has ever been. It has been my burden and I've wondered at times where God was when the pain was at its worst, but it has also been what makes me special. I would not have learned the things I've learned in the last many years if not for the misery of chronic pain. I would not have searched for my Savior or clung as tightly to him and God's biblical promises if I weren't tormented by my physical ailment. I would not be as close to the Lord as I am today if not for the days and nights of anguish that have molded me into the shape God wanted me to be, despite my doubts.

I, at the same moment, hate and love my pain. It's the burden that leads me to doubt, question, and grow. It's the hardship that makes me marvel at how beautiful he is. It's the conduit of God's grace that has forced me at times to be uncertain of his goodness. It has been my invitation to seek him, and while it has been hard, there has also been great joy in the hunt.

Hear me on this, though. I'm not saying that you need to go through something chronic like what I'm going through in order to grow in Christ. Although I think it's fair to say that every Christian will suffer (Philippians 1:29; 1 Peter 2:20–21) and that these sufferings are going to be one of our greatest catalysts for maturity in Christ, not everyone experiences the same trials to the same degree for the same duration. What's important is to run to God during our sufferings, instead of assuming he's absent or doesn't care. Don't waste your pain; use it as an opportunity to grow. Ask the hard questions in the process of your struggles. Lean into the confusion about why things are the way they are, under the blanket of faith that God knows exactly what he's doing and he loves you more abundantly than you can ever imagine.

I never would've thought that a run-in with a Texas Longhorn cow right outside the Austin airport would develop into a metaphor of such significance in my life, but here I am. Filtering my experiences through the avenue of Scripture, it's fun to see God wink at me in the seemingly mundane. I love that about him, and I'm thankful he cares enough about me to torment me with my heavy and beautiful "horns."

Reflection Questions

1. Have you ever been afraid to ask certain questions because of how you might be perceived by others? Where can you find a safe place to ask your questions (friend, family member, church, mentor, etc.)?

2. How can a perceived absence of God actually be a request to enter into the joy of searching after him?

3. What kinds of things can you do, think, feel, pray, journal, or say in order to use your pain as an opportunity to grow spiritually?

CHAPTER NINE

God Can, God Cares

Because he has spent his entire professional life in full-time ministry, a good friend and mentor of mine, Dan Flynn, has a number of talks he's given to college students. One of my favorites that he gives is entitled "God Can, God Cares." Thematically, the message is exactly what it sounds like—God is able to do anything, and he has personal interest and concern for you. That being said, at times over the years I have doubted both of those two points. Why? Because life's circumstances can be awfully damning evidence against God's love and capability to get things done. Often, our suffering can easily lead to doubt.

I met Brett, one of my best friends, when I was a campus minister and he was a sophomore at James Madison University. Brett was born with a rare condition that gave him chronic pancreatitis. His diet was completely affected by it, allowing him to consume only a very small amount of fat per day. Nothing he ate could be cooked in oil or butter, and every fat gram he consumed was tallied. Frequently and at often inconvenient times, Brett would have a flare-up, throwing him into excruciating pain and immediate fasting. He would have to go for days without eating anything just to ease the pain of the flare-up, and then slowly work his way back into his normal scrutinized eating routine. I was with him many times a flare-up happened, and hated seeing him in such pain that I couldn't at all help to improve.

Not long after Brett got married, he told me that he was going to go through a (at that time) unique medical procedure that extracted certain enzymes from his pancreas and injected them into his liver. His pancreas could then be removed, and his liver would act like a two-in-one organ. I had no idea this was even possible! The immediate result, though, was that he would become a type-one diabetic on the operating table.

That's right: literally overnight, Brett went from eating almost no fat ever to eating whatever fatty foods he wanted, but now had to constantly monitor his blood sugar and give himself insulin injections. Through it all, Brett has had an amazing trust and reliance on the Lord, but he's been no stranger to questioning God's methods as he's suffered.

Much like my own battle with physical suffering that I unpacked for you last chapter, Brett's life of consistent pain has become the overarching theme of his day-to-day. Brett probably never would have assumed that his physical issues would be the main plot of his story and characterize the way he processes his doubts, his Christian faith, and his foundational beliefs concerning the nature of God. If he had to choose from a list of things that the Lord would use to develop him as a believer, I don't think he would have ever chosen physical pain and suffering.

Yet Brett isn't in charge of his life—and rightly so, because he has been purchased by God and he belongs to the Lord. God can do with Brett what he pleases. As Scripture insists, "[D]o you not know that your body is a temple of the Holy Spirit within you, whom you have from God? You are not your own, for you were bought with a price. So glorify God in your body" (1 Corinthians 6:19–20). Simply put, we're slaves to God through the blood of Jesus Christ. He is our master, and we must trust in his plan for our lives. Yet as simple as this is to say, it's quite a different thing to believe when it seems like God is not really able to remove our suffering and/or he doesn't really care that we're suffering.

Rarely does a person choose indifference when the fires of life start to burn hot, and if we aren't prepared, the fire can be an easy path toward bitterness, anger, and resentment of God for what he has "done to us."[1] Consequently, it's important that we start with some biblical examples, from which we can build a framework for how to look at life when we're tempted to doubt God's ability to help us in our need and care for us when we suffer.

God Can Do All Things

Probably the most famous biblical example that candidly addresses this topic is Ephesians 3:20–21: "Now to him who is able to do far more abundantly than all that we ask or think, according to the power at work within us, to him be glory in the church and in Christ Jesus throughout all generations, forever and ever. Amen." God is able to do far more than what we ask or even *think*? That's quite expansive. I can think of a lot. Words certainly have the ability to help us understand profound truths, and Paul pulls no punches in this passage. He unapologetically emphasizes that God *can* do more.

However, the broken world we live in, our unredeemed flesh, and the devil can easily tempt us to believe that God isn't able to do all things. I won't speak for you, but in my weaker moments I've certainly had thoughts that angrily fly in the face of Ephesians 3.*Oh, you're able to do far more than all I ask or think, God? Well, all evidence in my life right now is entirely to the contrary.* Doubt can certainly fuel the fire of cynicism and jadedness.

But coming to the heart-level conclusion that my doubts are almost always borne out of my difficult circumstances—and are mostly knee-jerk reactions to how I'm feeling during my misery—helps erase those doubts in light of the truth of God's Word. Sure, I might feel like God can't take my suffering away, but that doesn't mean my feelings are correct. When we're hurting, our emotions are influenced in a myriad of ways. We'll be tempted to allow our emotions to dictate reality to us. Even though we know emotions can be powerful, let's not forget that they come and go. Scripture must always outweigh our feelings, no matter how strong they might be, because the erratic nature of emotion is never a good foundation for making decisions.

When I'm doubting that God can, the Bible reminds me that my doubts are unwarranted. Scripture tells us that nothing is too hard for God (Jeremiah 32:17, 27), that he can do all things (Mark 14:36), and that no purpose of his can be thwarted (Job 42:2). There is a comfort in this truth that feels like a warm blanket over me, especially when the circumstances of life feel contrastingly awful and chaotic. Often the root of my doubt lies in a mistrust of God and his character. The Bible—unlike any other book—is able to realign my heart and put me back on the correct path of faith in the Lord and trust in his Word. The Bible is crystal clear about the fact that we can know and understand God's powerful ability to do anything (see Matthew 19:26; Luke 1:37), and this is made no more obvious than in the cross of Christ.

Knowing and believing in the central figure of Scripture makes it possible to see in a real and tangible way that God *can*, because he *already did*—through the life, death, and resurrection of Jesus Christ. Where sin once separated sinful man from God, Christ reconciles us with the Father through faith. Dwelling on this beautiful good news pulls our gaze away from the gloom of doubt in God's ability and toward the hope of faith in him, because of Christ's atoning sacrifice on behalf of humanity. The gospel drives the point home, once and for all, that God can. I'm reminded of the point made by J. D. Greear, "[God], as I pray, I'll measure your compassion by the cross and your power by the resurrection."[2]

In light of the fact that God is able, we can also see that God cares—again, definitively—because of Jesus.

God Cares about Us

Suffering can surely cause someone to doubt the fact that God cares about us, as we learn about in the story of Shadrach, Meshach, and

Abednego. This is one of the most famous Old Testament stories that many a child has heard if they happened to have grown up attending Sunday school.

These three Jewish exiles in Babylon, under the rule of King Nebuchadnezzar, refuse to bow down to a golden idol the king has made; because of their loyalty to the only true God, they're thrown into a fiery furnace. The furnace is so hot that it kills the guards who throw the men in—but once the king looks inside the furnace, he sees not three men but four figures walking around calmly in the fire, unbound and unharmed.

It's the fourth person who catches the king's attention, because he looks like a superhero of some kind, and it's clear that the fourth man is the reason the other three aren't dead. Scripture says Nebuchadnezzar refers to the appearance of the fourth man as one who is like a "son of the gods" (Daniel 3:25). If you do any commentary reading, you'll learn that many believe this "son of the gods" is in fact *the* Son of God, Jesus Christ. Yes, Jesus Christ—right here in the Old Testament. Keller explains,

> The fiery, divine friend is a vivid commentary on Isaiah 43:3, 5—"When you walk through the fire, you will not be burned; the flames shall not set you ablaze. . . . Do not be afraid for I will be with you." Who would have ever expected how concretely God was speaking when he said, "I will be *with* you in the fire?" Do you see the infinite lengths to which he went to be with us? When we remember that Jesus had been living in unimaginable glory and bliss for all eternity, we realize that his entire life was, for him, like walking in a furnace.[3]

All of Christ's life was lived under stress. He was constantly misunderstood (John 6:59–66), often attacked by people seeking to kill him (Luke 4:29), and even rejected by his closest friends (John 18:17, 25–27). And as he died on the cross, he truly entered our deserved furnace. He was condemned unjustly to a painful death, and he went through it all by himself. As Keller says,

"When the fire of God's wrath burned him to the core and blazed unchecked over him, he was entirely alone."[4]

But why? Because on the cross, Jesus was suffering not only *with* us as a human being but *for* us as an atoning sacrifice. If you remember that he was thrown into the ultimate furnace *for* you, you can begin to sense him in your smaller furnaces *with* you.[5]

See, God understands. He knows firsthand what it's like to live through the miseries of this world. As a result, we can know for sure that he is near when we hurt, available to be depended on within our hardships. God cares, and the proof of his concern and love is in the suffering of Jesus so that we can live. No other proof is needed. The cross ends all debates about whether or not God cares about the human race.

When I'm suffering and feeling lonely, the cross helps me know that I'm not alone, because Jesus went through it too. He understands loneliness on a cosmic level because on the cross, for the first time in eternity, God the Son was no longer in fellowship with God the Father. On the cross, the Father turned his face away from his Son, leaving Jesus completely and utterly alone. As Martin Luther said, "God forsaking God. What man can understand this?"[6] All the earth had rejected him—there is nothing lonelier than that.

When you're doubting God's love, look to the cross. When you're questioning his affection, look to the cross. When you're searching for his devotion to you, look to the cross. Jesus holds the remedy to our doubt in his nail-scarred hands. Knowing this in our heads and believing this in our hearts will drastically alter the wrestling match with doubt.

As Christians, we're not deists. Deism is the belief that God created the world, people, and all the things in it, but remains uninvolved and uninterested in the affairs of his creation. God built the race car, so to speak, but has no interest in driving it.

I know it can be hard to believe that God can and God cares during our trials, and sometimes it can be easier to reconcile one's self to deism than accommodate a loving, sovereign God. But the cross of Jesus Christ blows that doubt to pieces once we open our eyes and truly see what he did for us at "The Place of the Skull,"

Golgotha (John 19:17). The cross undermines all of our doubt and insists that we can be sure the all-powerful, mighty God can and did go to infinite lengths just to be with us.

Turn your eyes upon Jesus. Look full in his wonderful face. And the doubts of your heart will grow strangely dim in the light of his glory and grace.[7]

Reflection Questions

1. Is it difficult to believe God is able to do anything and that he has personal interest and concern for you? If so, why?

2. How has your doubt of God's ability to do anything fueled the fire of jadedness and cynicism in your life? What steps can you take to instead shift your perspective to one of trust?

3. In what ways has your forgetfulness of Christ's sufferings led you to believe that God doesn't care about you? Be vulnerable and honest.

CHAPTER TEN

Work Through Your Doubts

I'm familiar with the feeling of just barely hanging on when my faith seems stretched to its limits. My chronic pain has done this to me repeatedly.

But Isaiah 42:3 says, "a bruised reed he will not break, and a faintly burning wick he will not quench; he will faithfully bring forth justice." Even when we're barely hanging on as an injured reed or faintly burning wick, so to speak, God will not break us. He will not snuff us out. He wants us to pursue him. He wants us to keep walking to him. It's important not to do the opposite and celebrate or revere doubt.

There have been many celebrities in the Christian spotlight who've become famous for constantly asking questions without ever approaching answers. They've made it cool to doubt and even celebrate the fact that they're doubters.[1] They're tantamount to the kid in the back of the classroom who's too cool to know or do anything definitive because their attitude about everything is basically "whatever." But doubt should never be something regarded as virtuous. We should never grow so comfortable with our doubt that it turns into a celebration.[2] Remember, every guest in your home is eventually supposed to leave. Doubt should never take up permanent residence in the home of your heart, because when it does you'll live your life in a way that never really takes God seriously. Your attitude and life will embody a "whatever" kind of stance.

Doubt isn't something to glorify; it's something to work through. G. K. Chesterton said, "Merely having an open mind is nothing. The object of opening the mind, as of opening the mouth, is to shut it again on something solid."[3] In other words, if you keep your mouth open long enough without biting down on something solid to eat, you're eventually going to starve. Likewise, if your mind is open for too long without closing down on something solid, it will eventually starve as well.

The one who doubts is like a wave tossed around by the wind; he or she is unstable (James 1:6–8). Living in a repeated state of instability with nothing firm to grab hold of in life is awful, and the Christian life is not meant to be lived this way. We have the ability to bite down on something solid in our faith. We can find stability beyond our constant questioning and coinciding confusion if we lean into our faith and trust that God will come through, alleviating our dark doubts.

Wallowing

Many Christians are far too easily pleased with a laid-back, doubtful attitude about life. It's easy to simply coast on a wave of doubt that never really gets you anywhere. But doubt should never be an excuse to justify passive sinful behavior or laziness, especially when it comes to clear biblical instruction that we shouldn't do so. As Hebrews 10:26–27 says, "[I]f we go on sinning deliberately after receiving the knowledge of the truth, there no longer remains a sacrifice for sins, but a fearful expectation of judgment, and a fury of fire that will consume the adversaries." Yikes. We're not going to get into the specifics of what "a fury of fire that will consume the adversaries" means right now, but instead focus on the "sinning deliberately" part.

The writer of Hebrews gives us a clear warning about sinning once you know the truth. Some men and women want to wallow in their doubts in order to justify a casual approach to

God and his command to live in holiness. This isn't only unwise but dangerous.

One might say, "I have my doubts about God's judgment and wrath. That doesn't seem to fit with a loving and forgiving God, so I don't really have to live the way the Bible says I should live." An apathetic attitude like this justifies sin and spits in the face of God's authority. Sitting in my doubt and claiming I don't know what to do is not at all a valid excuse. Knowing the right thing to do and not doing it is sin, plain and simple (James 4:17). Doubt isn't a virtue, and to pursue it or consistently wallow in it is wrong because it should never be used as a rationalization for ungodly behavior.

Instead, we should be men and women of intentionality and integrity. Yes, we can ask questions; and as we've already covered, the Bible gives us lots of room to doubt. But why take a nonchalant posture toward eternally weighty things? If you want to get a job somewhere, you don't just walk into the lobby of that business and stand around in sweatpants, waiting for someone to walk over to you and offer you employment. No, you work on your résumé, you fill out a job application, you set up an interview, you buy the appropriate business attire and get cleaned up. You remind yourself to keep eye contact and sit up straight when you're being evaluated by the boss, and you do whatever it takes to get that job offer.

How much more important is God than business employment? We need to attack our doubts with fervor. We need to move intentionally toward answers to the questions that make us feel stuck in our faith. Proactively working through our doubts and bombarding them with intentionality is the mature and godly approach to take, because of what's on the line. The importance of this can't be overstated, so let's work through our doubts with enthusiasm instead of indifference.

We Can Overcome

One of the most famous pieces of Scripture in all the Bible is Psalm 23:1–4. As the poet-shepherd David writes,

The LORD is my shepherd; I shall not want.
He makes me lie down in green pastures.
He leads me beside still waters.
He restores my soul.
He leads me in paths of righteousness
for his name's sake.
Even though I walk through the valley of the shadow of death,
I will fear no evil,
for you are with me;
your rod and your staff,
they comfort me.

This is encouraging, because we know we're not alone. Though you may walk through the valley of the shadow of death, you don't have to die there.[4] God himself walks through it with you. As a result, your doubt can be overcome.

Keep in mind that like most anything in life, overcoming your doubts will probably take time. As you walk through them, the process will be just that—a process. When we expect the wrestling match to end quickly, it can be easy to get discouraged and give up, settling on the mindset of, "Well, I guess this is just the way things are going to be indefinitely." But we should never settle on camping there. We don't want to build a home in the valley, because the valley is no place to set up residence for an undetermined amount of time. As Christians we move on from our doubt. We work through them, all the while holding onto the belief that God is going to show up and meet us as we work.

First John 5:4–5 says, "For everyone who has been born of God overcomes the world. And this is the victory that has overcome the world—our faith. Who is it that overcomes the world except the one who believes that Jesus is the Son of God?" It's clear to me that these verses are saying that the method we use to work through and conquer our doubt is faith.

Faith isn't the absence of doubt. Rather, faith in the Son of God is the means by which we can overcome and walk through the valley of doubt. Faith gives us the power to press on during the lengthy battles when we are weary and beat down. Faith helps us to see that though we walk in the valley, God is present and making us stronger. As we encounter the diseases of doubt that strike against us, we develop antibodies to help us fight the inevitable future battles that come our way.[5] Tim Keller uses this metaphor deftly when he writes, "A faith without some doubts is like a human body without antibodies in it. People who blithely go through life too busy or indifferent to ask hard questions about why they believe as they do will find themselves defenseless against either the experience of tragedy or the probing questions of a smart skeptic."[6]

Keller essentially argues that we need some doubts in our lives. We need to encounter them because when we fight them, we become stronger in our faith. The battle with doubt itself builds up antibodies in our system, preparing us for the certainty of future hardships. The faith that encounters doubt will become a sturdy, long-lasting faith to prop ourselves up against when life attacks.

Seeking answers when we doubt establishes health and strength in the Lord. Use the weapon of faith to work through your doubt, and wait to see God show up in ways that create a tighter bond in your relationship with him unlike anything you've ever experienced.

Think

It's a commonly held position within our culture that a doubter or skeptic is a person who thinks deeply. Consequently, it's also relatively normal to assume that a person of faith is someone who chooses *not* to think and just believe without using his or her brain.

I've heard unbelievers on the college campus use verses like 2 Corinthians 5:7 as a weapon against Christians to prove that we don't think the way we should, and that if we actually chose to use reason instead of lean on faith, we'd be persuaded away from the "silly" worldview that is Christianity. But when the apostle Paul writes, "we walk by faith, not by sight" (2 Corinthians 5:7), notice that he doesn't at all contrast faith with reason; he contrasts faith with sight.

Under the Knife

I heard a sermon once that reminded me of an experience I had at the doctor's office.[7] Less than a year ago, I discovered a bump on the back part of my neck, just below my hairline. It started small but then got bigger and bigger to the point that I needed to go in and get it checked out. There was no pain associated with it; I just noticed it was getting bigger. Initially, my doctor said it looked like a small cyst but that he wasn't 100 percent certain; he was going to have to take it out and have the growth tested to make sure it wasn't cancerous. I asked what kind of procedure something like that would require, and he assured me the process wouldn't be significant. Right there in the office, he would inject a local anesthetic, make a small incision on my neck, remove the growth, and then sew me back up with two or three stitches. The entire procedure would take less than fifteen minutes; it would be, as he called it, "simple enough for an intern to do it."

While I'm positive he was saying that just to help me relax, I assure you it did just the opposite. I had a ton of nervous questions for him. He answered them all casually, doubling down on the fact that it was an easy removal, and other than a slight burning sensation where they'd inject the local anesthetic it would be pain-free. He helped me think through all the facts, and as I gathered information about the truth of the minor surgery I felt much better. He convinced me it wouldn't be a big deal, so I made an appointment to come back in a week and have the growth removed.

I had faith that my doctor was telling the truth. I was convinced—until I arrived the next week and saw the scalpels and syringes resting on a little tray in my exam room. I saw the examination table with that crinkly sounding hard butcher paper pulled out over it. I saw the nurse come in and put on latex gloves, and my doctor enter the room wearing his white lab coat. All of a sudden, my nervous doubts bubbled to the surface, and I had to ask myself where they were coming from. I started to lose my faith and question why I was doing this in the first place.

As I think back on this event, I can now clearly see that my doubts were not coming from new evidence. They weren't coming from new reasons or lines of thought, but from my sight. I was losing faith in my doctor and this "simple procedure," not because of thinking or reasoning more but because of the sight of the scalpels, the sight of the needles, and the sight of my environment. In the doctor's office that day, things looked awful, so I lost my faith. But what did I need to do in order to regain it?

Simply put, I needed to work through my doubts and think. Doubt wasn't about thinking more, but thinking less! I needed to remind myself of why I was doing this. I needed to remember that my doctor was a trustworthy and skilled physician. I needed to ponder about all the things I was told the previous week—I needed to work it through and renew my thinking. My doubts and fears were coming from an absence of thinking and just reacting to what I saw around me that day.

See, things that are true don't always seem or feel true. In order to regain and keep my faith in the truth when doubts come, I have to keep renewing my thinking and work it through. It's often not the thinking that destroys our faith, it's the sight.

Consider and Understand

During the Sermon on the Mount, Jesus talked to a group of anxious people, and he exhorts them by saying, "And why are you anxious about clothing? *Consider* the lilies of the field, how they grow: they neither toil nor spin, yet I tell you, even Solomon in all his glory was not arrayed like one of these. But if God so clothes the grass of the field, which today is alive and tomorrow is thrown into the oven, will he not much more clothe you, O you of little faith?" (Matthew 6:28–30, emphasis added). Jesus says here that in order to gain faith, we must *consider* the lilies and see how God takes care of them. Since we are much more valuable to God than flowers or grass or birds, God will take care of us. Work it through and think intentionally about these facts. Consider it. Reason with it. Deduce the truth.

People with little or no visible faith are people who just react and don't think. They let their feelings and emotions harass them; the circumstances of their lives corner and oppress them. It takes thought to have faith. When in doubt, don't think less and let circumstances push you further and further into doubt. Work through your doubts and think more. Remember how God has worked in your past. Think about when he came through time and time again for his people in Scripture. Reflect on his kindness and love for you despite your ever-present rebellion. Consider and allow thoughtful, truth-saturated reasoning to strengthen your faith, because your faith should be rooted in thought.

To be a person of faith is to think more and comprehend the realities of truth all around us. Work through, grasp, fathom, discern, consider, understand—*think!* Doubt will pull you from thought, but faith will lead you to use your God-given brain more deeply. This isn't a popular opinion among skeptics looking from the outside in on Christianity, so it's important to visibly and vocally live the reality of walking by faith as we stay grounded in thought.

Reflection Questions

1. How have lingering on or glorifying your doubts led your heart away from God instead of toward him?

2. The idea of doubt working as an antibody in your spiritual life is unique but profound. How have your past doubts worked as antibodies in your life, to help prepare you for the more difficult aspects of life and faith?

3. How are faith and thought related? How can more intentional thinking strengthen your faith?

CHAPTER ELEVEN

Greener Grass

You've probably heard someone use a version of the cliché, "The grass looks greener on the other side of the fence." Essentially, it means that other people may *seem* to be in a better situation than you, but in reality their situation may not be as good as it seems. I don't know of anyone who hasn't struggled at some point with thinking or feeling that they'd have it better if they were in someone else's shoes. But when a human being is in some kind of distress or disorder, he or she often compares the *worst* of what they are experiencing to the *best* of someone else's life. For example, singles who want to be married often compare their loneliness to a married couple's companionship—measuring the most difficult parts of singleness with the greatest parts of marriage.

This kind of comparison is natural, but unwise. In our worst moments, we might think that because we're experiencing a substantial doubt, it would simply be easier to abandon belief altogether. But be careful not to, as Emma and Glen Scrivener put it, "look wistfully at your unbelieving friends as though they don't have to bother with faith."[1]

Why? Because everyone has faith in something—everyone. Tim Keller puts it like this in his book *Making Sense of God*: "You can't doubt belief A except on the basis of some belief B you are believing instead at the moment. So, for example, you cannot say, 'No one can know enough to be certain about God and religion,' without assuming at that moment that you know enough about the nature of religious knowledge to be certain about *that*."[2] Keller is essentially saying that faith is everywhere. Even though the skeptic or atheist might not label what she believes "faith," the means by which she makes decisions is based on trust in a worldview and fundamental set of assumptions about her existence. She might argue with you over the semantics of it, but the bottom line is that everyone—believer or unbeliever—has faith.

We all rely on systems and foundations we can't see or prove; as a result, all of us are placing our faith somewhere. As Emma and Glen Scrivener explain about the faith of the unbeliever, "We all take for granted the regularity of the universe, the reliability of our senses, and the rationality of our minds. We appeal to ultimate values like goodness, truth, beauty, and love. None of these can be proved scientifically; they're all matters of faith. But without Christ, they have no true, beautiful, and loving foundation. If you think *you're* having a crisis of faith, you can be sure it's nothing compared to the crisis of faith that is atheism."[3]

This thought is significant, as it helps us to understand what is true when it comes to faith. There aren't two camps—people who have faith and people who don't. Rather, everyone who has ever walked the planet is in the same category. We're all trusting in something. Therefore, the natural line of logic leads us next to the question, "Who or what is the object of my faith?"

Resting on Jesus

From the beginning of this book, we've seen that doubt isn't the same thing as unbelief. Unbelief, as Keller argues, is a conclusion someone reaches based on faith in that certain "Belief B."

As Christians, our faith rests on Jesus, but when doubt rears its ugly head we might think that the way to deal with it is to somehow muster up more faith. But why would we try to muster up more faith when Jesus says things like, "If you had faith like a grain of mustard seed, you could say to this mulberry tree, 'Be uprooted and planted in the sea,' and it would obey you" (Luke 17:6)?

Scripture seems to clearly indicate that the Christian only needs a tiny bit of faith to see wondrous things happen, not a five-ton truck of it. You might be asking then, "So what exactly is faith if, according to Jesus, so little of it is needed to work through my doubts?" Good question—I'm glad I thought of it for you. Again, Emma and Glen Scrivener helpfully explain that the answer isn't as complicated as we might make it out to be:

> Faith is simply resting on Jesus. . . . Since [it is], in times of doubt I don't need more 'faith,' I need more Jesus. And when I get more Jesus—through preaching, Scripture, sacraments, prayer, community—then, maybe even in spite of myself, my faith is revived.
>
> When we focus on the *him* of Jesus rather than the *what* of "faith," doubts are reduced, relativized, replaced, and even redeemed. It might just be that the path of doubt was God's way of bringing you to a deeper, richer knowledge of Jesus himself.[4]

We forget so often that the gospel is the answer. Deeply rooting our hearts in the truth of God's radical love for humanity isn't a personal *effort* thing, it's a *person* thing—and that person is Jesus. The gospel isn't just something we as Christians accept and then move on to more "important" or "advanced" things; it's something we need on a minute-by-minute basis, and the something we need is him. We never graduate from the gospel. We need Jesus to save us, we need him now to live the Christian life, and we will need him in the future on into eternity.

Let's never forget the importance of looking to him to find the answer. It's not more effort, strategies, five-step plans, or problem-solving ability. Faith itself isn't the quantitative measure of how we're doing in our walk with God when doubt comes along. If that were true, Jesus wouldn't have said that it need only to be the size of a mustard seed. Rather, faith is the means to the end, and the end is Christ himself.

When we glorify or focus on measurable aspects of faith (e.g., "just have more faith!"), being a Christian gets reduced to a religious bartering system between humanity and God. "I have more faith, so God gives me more blessing," one might believe. But if we think that having more faith makes it more likely that the Lord will bless us and eliminate our doubts, our focus is off. Being a Christian is being in relationship with God through Jesus Christ—he should be our focus, and all it takes is a mustard seed–sized faith to experience that relationship. The goal is Christ and Christ alone, and we are called to rest on him when doubts spring up. Faith is an important part of all this, but faith is not the end goal, Jesus is.

When your faith feels in crisis because of your lingering doubts, use the tiny tool of faith to get more Jesus. As my close friend Dan Flynn always says, "Keep your eye on the ball. Jesus is the ball."

The greenest grass of all is resting in Jesus, even when we're struggling with questions and doubt. Nothing can satisfy like a relationship with him, so let's rest in Christ and allow the gospel to make our hearts content because faith is hard.

Reflection Questions

1. When was a time that you looked longingly at the "other side of the fence" and believed there were greener pastures away from following Christ?

2. Why is the Christian life simply resting in Jesus?

3. Because faith is hard, why is the answer “more Jesus” and not “more faith”?

CHAPTER TWELVE

Fight Back

We've already talked at length about how doubt can be incredibly debilitating when it comes to your relationship with the Lord. In fact, if we are not careful and don't take the proper steps in our walks with God, unbelief can be just around the corner.

I've certainly had a few missteps on my journey over the last twenty years in ministry with young people. There have been times when I really wanted to believe that I was a new creation, but when the months passed and I hadn't seen the Holy Spirit change my life or mold my hardened heart into something pliable that God could use, I was unable to believe God's promise that "he who began a good work in you will bring it to completion at the day of Jesus Christ" (Philippians 1:6). The apostle Paul seemed to be pretty sure that God could bring about change, but there certainly have been times when I didn't share Paul's confidence.

Regardless of my state of mind or attitude of heart, though, there is one thing that comforts me when I don't understand the confusing elements of life: no matter how great my doubt, God is greater. It's true; let me give you an example.

Thomas once boldly said after the other disciples had told him about the resurrected Christ, "Unless I see in his hands the mark of the nails, and place my finger into the mark of the nails, and place my hand into his side, I will never believe" (John 20:25).

Never? I mean, really? I will *never* believe? That's an audacious thing to say after you've spent three years alongside the Messiah during his public ministry, seeing firsthand the kinds of things he could do—not to mention that Jesus himself had said he was going to rise from the dead after he was killed.

But this is what Thomas said, and of course Jesus eventually came through for him. A little over a week later, Jesus showed up face-to-face with Thomas, and the doubter's heart was convinced. Jesus then went on to say to him, "Have you believed because you have seen me? Blessed are those who have not seen and yet have believed" (John 20:29). Thomas's doubt was great, but God was greater.

The Lord is never repulsed by our doubt. In fact, he pursues us even when we question him. Sometimes when things get bad and doubts rise to the surface, the things that are true don't feel true. God's love, grace, sovereignty, and existence are more real than we can ever fathom, but it certainly doesn't feel that way from time to time. But just because, for example, God's love doesn't seem to be true it doesn't mean our assumptions are correct. And in the middle of all that, Jesus says, "Blessed are you who have not seen and yet have believed." It's encouraging to know that when I just don't get it, God is always greater.

Practical Strategies

I think it's important for me to share a few realistic things with you, in order to help you get on the solution side of life when it comes to the battle with doubt. I'm a practical guy, so application is often what I gravitate to when I read or hear something that inspires me. So if you're feeling trapped in a seemingly endless spiral of theories about how to treat your doubt, this chapter will probably click with you.

I'm going to walk us through four things that can act as weapons to help in the fight with the kind of doubt that leads to dark places. My hope is that as you battle, many of these weapons (or at least one) will help you see victory and come out on the other side stronger in the Lord than when you went in as your doubts started.

1. Practice Thankfulness

The antidote to many of the doubts that can darken my life has been an intentional movement toward dwelling on all I'm thankful for. In a real sense, thankfulness renews your mind and refreshes your heart in ways that make it nearly impossible to ruminate on doubt. Paul David Tripp puts this astutely:

> It is exactly at the point when you are tempted to think that you're not blessed that counting your blessings is the most important. A thankful heart is the best defense against a doubting heart. . . . As a defense against doubt, it is really important to give yourself to quiet moments when you look at the trail behind you and what is now around you for evidences that God is good and worthy of your trust.[1]

Just like Israel, we are incredibly forgetful of the miraculous ways God has worked in our lives. In all likelihood, there are multiple examples of God's provision, presence, and care you've experienced that you could probably recall if you simply took the time to think about them. And after you remember, rejoice. Praise God for how he's worked, and watch your focus shift from dark doubt to bright thankfulness.

Each week on Sunday, my family pauses to do family devotions (or what my then-four-year-old daughter called "demotions"). We read through a kid's Bible study, ask questions, pray, and sing worship songs. But my favorite part of family devotions is when we do the thankfulness jar. All four of us get a slip of paper and a colored marker, and we write down the thing or things we're thankful for in the last week, add our name and the date, and then share it with each other. After we all have our turn, we fold the paper in half and slip it into a big mason jar with a slit on the lid. It's been a great way to dwell on God's love and work in our lives, and also a fun way to see the thankfulness we share build up in that jar over time.

Practicing thankfulness is incredibly soothing to a life agitated by doubts. We refocus our hearts on the giver of all good things and not on the circumstances that never seem to be quite good enough for our thirsty hearts. When we drink from the fountain of living water, we worship with gratitude instead of agonizing over our doubts.

2. Get with the Real and Right People

I've touched on this a little bit already, but it's always important to be reminded that you cannot battle your doubts as an isolated island, at least not with any sustained amount of success. Despite what our individualistic culture may push, Christianity isn't a solo thing. This is why it's vital to plug in with a body of believers in a local church and campus ministry.

I know in a world of earbuds and custom-order everything, good community seems impossible, but I promise you that it's worth pursuing—especially when you're wrestling with doubt. I also know that it can feel like you're in community simply because you're surrounded by people all the time, whether you're a student or in the working world. But real relationships require depth in a way that proximity alone won't accomplish.

Likewise, don't assume that because you're well connected via text and social media, you're living in community. Church and authentic Christian camaraderie happen in the context of face-to-face interaction. If we know a person solely through the veneer of social media profiles and edited text messages, we don't know that person entirely. Sure, we can begin to understand who a person is by reading what they appreciate, what kind of entertainment they enjoy, and what restaurant they'd like to eat at this weekend, but that is only part of the picture. We're deceiving ourselves if we think we can get to know someone deeply only through social media.[2] You were created for something much deeper.

The real you is the real you, and you shouldn't want people to only experience the polished version of you. So when you doubt, do it alongside real human beings. As things progress the way God created them to in the human relational experience, others will eventually see through the shine of your edited self—and that's when real change, help, hope, and growth happens.

Genuine relationships can't happen to the degree you need and long for through digital avenues. It'll always lack depth because it can never be a substitute for the real thing. My friend and coworker Keri Armentrout puts it this way: "Social media should never be a substitute for relationships, but a springboard for relationships."

Let's never forget the value of getting with the right people as we struggle with doubt. There is no good substitute for the real thing, so find your people and walk with Jesus as a group in order to see your doubt defeated.

3. Continually Remind Yourself of the Gospel

One of the best ways to fight back against doubt is to repeatedly remind yourself of the truth. There is a hypnotizing effect that our culture can have on us as it attempts to sway us to unbelief. Social media, advertising, YouTube, movies, television, radio, podcasts, magazines—practically everything, all the time, is pushing us away from God.

Consequently, if you don't spend consistent time renewing your mind with the gospel, you'll give in to culture's push and abandon Christ. Each of us must gaze into the beauty of the gospel if we're going to have a fighting chance to live in a way that honors God and shuns unbelief.

But what does it mean to gaze into the gospel? It's always a good idea to start first with regular time in God's Word. Scripture is how God chooses to communicate with us, so why would we ever treat something like that with apathy or take it for granted? Our perspective in life should be shaped by the Word, knowing that its central message is all about Jesus Christ.

The fact that God came down in the form of a human, lived a life of perfection, was executed unjustly, and conquered death in the resurrection is astounding. Even though we as Christians may have heard this over and over again, we should never grow tired of how magnificent the gospel is. When we truly grasp the lengths God went to in order to rescue us from our own rebellion, it snaps the binding ropes of doubt that have tied up our hearts.

The gospel is everything, and in it we wield the most powerful of all weapons to be used against doubt. Show me a heart that forgets the gospel, and I'll show you a life that is swallowed by the crushing effects of doubt. But show me a life that continually reminds itself of the truth of who Jesus is and who we are as a result of Jesus's work, and I'll show you a life of joy that is overwhelmed with God's goodness and love.

Preach the gospel to yourself at all times. Use words. Use actions. Drink deeply from the Scriptures and break free from the shackles of doubt.

4. Share Your Faith

Not only do we need to regularly preach the gospel to ourselves, but we also need to engage with others about the gospel on a steady basis too. I'm convinced that one of the best ways to counteract the offensive attacks of doubt in your life is to proactively communicate the gospel with others.

When we are adopted into God's family, we are given a new purpose beyond our personal relationship with the Lord. This purpose involves us being proactive about communicating our faith with others who need to hear about it. Sure, it's scary and risky. And every single time, it involves us killing the default comfort setting that seems so prevalent and powerful inside of our hearts.

Personally, I've never been 100 percent comfortable when I share my faith. Never. Maybe some other people have, but not me. I'll tell you this, though: I never feel more alive than when I do. When I communicate my faith, I'm excited, scared, happy, nervous, warm, and intimidated all at once. My mouth is usually dry, my armpits are usually wet, and my heart beats faster than when I'm on the elliptical for forty-five minutes. It's never easy for me, but regardless of how the conversation turns out I always seem to walk away with a renewed sense of purpose and energy. On more than one occasion after I've shared my faith, I've walked away and said aloud, "Man, I feel so alive right now."[3] Doubt is no match for that, because sharing the gospel is what we were made for. The Great Commission in Matthew 28:18–20 isn't just a charge for the "special" Christians—it's a charge to anyone who follows Christ. There is no junior varsity in God's kingdom.

As a follower of Jesus Christ, all of your life is not meant to be lived in the comfort of remaining silent about your faith. In fact, the discomfort that can come as a result of sharing your faith is a fantastic weapon against doubt. As we preach the gospel to others with love and care, we are reminded of God's love and care for us, pushing doubt out of our lives and awakening worship within our hearts.

Doubt is a battle worth fighting. And part of the reason it's worth fighting is because it's not just this battle that's at stake—it's also the battle for your future. If we aren't diligent to fight our doubts in an intentional way, the ripple effects can be disastrous. I'm not trying to scare you, but I do want you to see how important it is that we act and enthusiastically fight back.

Our God is a God of action. He's constantly working in our lives in a million different ways. And we're created in his image. So when doubts flood your heart and mind, fight. Don't just sit around and wait for the doubts to subside on their own; get proactive because it's about way more than just this battle. Your walk with God in the coming years could be on the line. A life that neglects its Maker is tragic indeed.

Reflection Questions

1. What are some specific things you're thankful for? Take some time right now to write down the things God has blessed you with over the course of your life.

2. What are some intentional choices you can make to remind yourself of the gospel each day?

3. Who are some of the nonbelievers in your life you'd be willing to share the gospel with? Make a plan about how to talk with them about the most important relationship in your life—your relationship with God.

Conclusion

There's this wild and somewhat bizarre story in Genesis 32:22–32, where the Bible tells us about Jacob wrestling with God. During my freshman year of college, I remember reading it as a brand-new Christian and being confused as to what was going on and what it all meant.

Jacob sends his family across a stream, and then ends up wrestling with God all night long until the sun comes up. At one point, Jacob's hip is touched by God during the wrestling match, throwing it out of socket. Jacob then clings to his opponent, the Lord, and God blesses him.

What has always interested me in this story is that verse 24 says that they wrestle, but then verse 26 says this: "Then he said, 'Let me go, for the day has broken.' But Jacob said, 'I will not let you go unless you bless me.'" Jacob goes from wrestling with God to clinging to God. From struggling to embracing. From fighting to cherishing. It's an obvious process right there in the text, but it's also easy to miss if you aren't looking for it. Since it's an odd story, we can let an important lesson slip through our fingers if we aren't careful. Jacob has moved from battling with God to grasping on to him in the hopes of receiving his blessing.

When we live with doubt, it quite often feels as if we're in the throes of a wrestling match with God. It can feel strange and embarrassing, sometimes even hopeless. But like our Bible story, our life's narrative should shift from wrestling to clinging, and that shift will often come via some sort of "hip socket moment" initiated by God. The wrestling match cannot go on forever. So instead of allowing your doubts to consume your faith, cling to God's legs and refuse to let go.

We needn't focus on the gloomy dark center of every silver-lined cloud that comes our way, but trust that the Lord can use our doubts to transform our lives and make us stronger than ever before. I encourage you: When your doubts arise (and they will), don't run away from the Lord; run to him. Cling to his feet. Perhaps you could even write out a doubting prayer to him on paper and ask him the questions that plague your heart when you lie awake in bed at night. Feel the freedom in your relationship with him to openly communicate that you just don't get it. Take your confusion, frustration, anger, and startled heart to God. In the process, watch the glory of the gospel become the Ebenezer, or "stone of help" (1 Samuel 7:12 NLT), to help you remember what he has done for you.

If there is any doubt in your heart that God loves you, just remind yourself of the length he went to in order to be in relationship with you. God slaughtered his one and only Son to reunite you to himself. As Tim Keller points out, "When Jesus looked down from the cross . . . he was in agony. He looked down at us—denying him, abandoning him, and betraying him—and in the greatest act of love in history, *he stayed*."[1]

Gazing into the beauty and complexity of the gospel helps us to overcome our doubts because it screams to us in a quiet whisper, "God loves you. He *has* to love you. Look at what he did to show his love for you."

Feed on this truth every day. The world is on a mission to disciple you into apathy about your relationship with God. If you aren't fighting that evil mission with the full strength of the good news found in Scripture, your doubts will swallow you whole and spit you out in the land of unbelief.

Don't fear your doubts; use them. Turn them into a tool that generates gospel health in your life along with the rich blessing of caring for others who are currently walking the path you used to trod. This is what it means to love the Lord your God with all your heart, soul, and mind—and to love your neighbor as yourself (Matthew 22:35–40).

For Further Reading

Here are a few apologetics books I can recommend as you study a defense of the Christian faith. There are, of course, numerous apologetics books to choose from, but this short list can get you started:

1. Timothy Keller, *The Reason for God: Belief in an Age of Skepticism* (New York: Viking, 2008).
2. Rebecca McLaughlin, *Confronting Christianity: 12 Hard Questions for the World's Largest Religion* (Wheaton, IL: Crossway, 2019).
3. Timothy Keller, *Making Sense of God: An Invitation to the Skeptical* (New York: Viking, 2016).
4. Josh McDowell and Sean McDowell, *More Than a Carpenter*, rev. ed. (Carol Stream, IL: Tyndale Momentum, 2009).
5. C. S. Lewis, *Mere Christianity* (New York: HarperCollins, 1952).
6. Lee Strobel, *The Case for Christ: A Journalist's Personal Investigation of the Evidence for Jesus* (Grand Rapids: Zondervan, 1998).

Acknowledgments

My friend Paul David Tripp encouraged me to write this book, because he believed that a voice was needed in the lives of young people who wrestle with doubt. Consequently, I owe him full credit for the idea to write this. Paul, in many ways you've changed my life. Thank you for your faithfulness to the gospel and your authenticity with me over these last few years. I love you, brother. Also, if you ever need any fashion tips, I'm your man.

* * *

There are certain people who, when you think of them, bring a smile to your face. My wife, Rachael, is one of those people. She has been a conduit of God's loving hand in my life, and I can't wait to see all the ways she'll make fun of me as I get older. Love you, babe. Thanks for being my best friend.

* * *

Rick James is one of the weirdest people I've ever met in my life, and I can't believe I get to spend time with someone who not only encourages me and my writing, but also models an active life of prayer, love for God's Word, and joy because of McDonald's breakfast. If it weren't for him, in many ways, I wouldn't be writing. I can't thank you enough for your influence in my life, Rick. Please stay bizarre.

* * *

In the last several years, I've had a number of great conversations with my friend Brian Barnett on the topic of doubt. He has been the source of much helpful insight when it comes to doubting well, along with the fact that he is a godly example of what it means to suffer and doubt while seeking Jesus. I'm continually in awe of how incredible you are, Brian. Thank you for your friendship, your example, and your unbridled passion for quality ice cream.

Endnotes

Introduction

1. Alister McGrath, "When Doubt Becomes Unbelief," *Tabletalk Magazine*, January 1, 1992, accessed January 31, 2020, https://www.ligonier.org/learn/articles/when-doubt-becomes-unbelief.

2. Michael Kruger, interviewed by Ryan Troglin, "How to Survive World Religions 101," *The Gospel Coalition* August 27, 2015, accessed January 31, 2020, https://www.thegospelcoalition.org/article/how-to-survive-world-religions-101.

Chapter 1

1. The John 10:10 Project, "Doubt and the Psalms," YouTube, May 9, 2017, 2:15, https://www.youtube.com/watch?v=fGzd-s7g0uw&t=10s.

2. The details of this story, along with the lyrics of this hymn, can be found in Christopher Knapp, *Who Wrote Our Hymns* (New York: Wilson Foundation, 1925).

3. Ibid.

4. Dan Hardesty, "What about All My Doubts? " (sermon), Community Church of Chesapeake, July 29, 2018, accessed January 31, 2020, http://www.ccconfire.org/sermons/what-about.

Chapter 2

1. George Müller, quoted in Roy B. Zuck, *The Speaker's Quote Book* (Grand Rapids: Kregel, 1997), 15.

Chapter 3

1. McGrath, "When Doubt Becomes Unbelief."
2. Ibid.
3. Adapted from Bill Bright, *Have You Made the Wonderful Discovery of the Spirit-filled Life?* (Orlando, FL: Cru Press, 2018).
4. "Trust and Obey," John H. Sammis, 1887, from *United Methodist Hymnal* (Nashville: The United Methodist Publishing House, 1989).

Chapter 5

1. McGrath, "When Doubt Becomes Unbelief."
2. Ibid.
3. Ibid.
4. Ibid.
5. Elizabeth Scott, "Rumination: Why Do People Obsess Over Things?" July 1, 2018, accessed January 31, 2020, https://www.verywellmind.com/rumination-why-do-people-obsess-over-things-3144571.
6. Ibid.
7. McGrath, "When Doubt Becomes Unbelief."
8. Ibid.
9. Josh McDowell and Sean McDowell, *More Than a Carpenter*, rev. ed. (Carol Stream, IL: Tyndale Momentum, 2009).
10. McGrath, "When Doubt Becomes Unbelief."
11. These thoughts come from my previous book *I Am a Tool: To Help with Your Dating Life* (Orlando, FL: Cru Press, 2014), 45–47.
12. http://www.thegospelcoalition.org and https://www.desiringgod.org, respectively.

Chapter 6

1. "At Close Range," "Jim Carrey Speech at the Golden Globe Awards 2016," January 12, 2016, 1:58, https://www.youtube.com/watch?v=a9J8GaeDqVc.
2. Alister McGrath, *The Twilight of Atheism: The Rise and Fall of Disbelief in the Modern World* (New York: Oxford University Press, 2004), 230.
3. Timothy Keller, *The Reason for God: Belief in an Age of Skepticism* (New York: Viking, 2008), 47.

Chapter 7

1. Bill Bright, *10 Basic Steps toward Christian Maturity*, reprint ed. (Orlando, FL: Cru Press, 2018). Also available online at https://www.cru.org/us/en/train-and-grow/10-basic-steps/5-the-bible.html.
2. See "For Further Reading" recommendations at the end of this book.

3. Bright, *10 Basic Steps toward Christian Maturity.*

4. Keller, *The Reason for God*, 202.

5. Thomas Arnold, *Christian Life—Its Hopes, Its Fears, and Its Close* (London: T. Fellowes, 1859), 324.

6. William Lane Craig, "Jesus: The Search Continues," The John Ankerberg Show. Available at https://www.jashow.org/resources/jesus-the-search-continues.

7. Josh McDowell, *Evidence That Demands a Verdict* (San Bernardino, CA: Campus Crusade for Christ International, 1973), 231.

8. Josh McDowell and Sean McDowell, *More Than a Carpenter.*

9. Keller, *The Reason for God*, 204.

10. N. T. Wright, *The Resurrection of the Son of God* (Minneapolis: Fortress, 2003), 608.

11. Keller, *The Reason for God*, 205–6.

12. N. T. Wright, *Who Was Jesus?* (Grand Rapids: Eerdmans, 1993), 63.

13. Keller, *The Reason for God*, 208.

14. See, among other passages, Matthew 16:21; 17:23; 20:19; 26:61; Mark 8:31; 10:34; Luke 9:22; 18:33; John 2:19. Also, after Christ died and rose, people and angels referred back to Jesus talking about his own resurrection in places like Matthew 28:6; 26:61; Luke 24:6–7.

Chapter 8

1. Russ Ramsey, in Jason Cook and Greg Thornbury, "How I've Dealt with Intellectual Doubts about Christianity," YouTube, posted by The Gospel Coalition, August 17, 2017, https://www.youtube.com/watch?v=cC8XBY_Tnyw.

2. Ibid.

3. Sheldon Vanauken, *A Severe Mercy*, reprint ed. (San Francisco: HarperOne, 2009).

4. Greg Thornbury, in Jason Cook and Greg Thornbury, "How I've Dealt with Intellectual Doubts about Christianity."

Chapter 9

1. A thought that, in its original form, was planted by Timothy Keller in *Walking with God through Pain and Suffering* (New York: Dutton, 2013).

2. J. D. Greear, *Gospel: Recovering the Power That Made Christianity Revolutionary* (Nashville: B&H, 2011).

3. Keller, *Walking with God through Pain and Suffering*, 233.

4. Ibid, 233–34, referencing Iain M. Duguid, *Daniel*, Reformed Expository Commentary (Philipsburg, NJ: P&R, 2008), 58.

5. Ibid, 235.

6. Martin Luther, cited in C. H. Spurgeon sermon, “The Saddest Cry from the Cross,” #2803, January 7, 1877, https://www.spurgeongems.org/sermon/chs2803.pdf.

7. Helen Howarth Lemmel, “Turn Your Eyes upon Jesus,” 1922. I replaced the lyric “things of earth” with “doubts of your heart” for specific emphasis.

Chapter 10

1. I’m mostly referring to individuals like Rob Bell.

2. Dan Hardesty, “What about All My Doubts?”

3. G. K. Chesterton, *The Autobiography of G.K. Chesterton* (San Francisco: Ignatius, 2006).

4. Hardesty, “What about All My Doubts?”

5. Ibid.

6. Keller, *The Reason for God*, xvi–xvii.

7. These thoughts were inspired by and borrowed from a sermon by Timothy Keller, “Noah and the Reasons of Faith; Faith as Understanding,” September 18, 1994, available at https://gospelinlife.com/downloads/noah-and-the-reasons-of-faith-faith-as-understanding-6350.

Chapter 11

1. Emma Scrivener and Glen Scrivener, “5 Things to Remember about Doubts,” *The Gospel Coalition*, October 8, 2018, accessed January 31, 2020, https://www.thegospelcoalition.org/article/doubt-doubts.

2. Timothy Keller, *Making Sense of God: An Invitation to the Skeptical* (New York: Viking, 2016), 38.

3. Scrivener and Scrivener, “5 Things to Remember about Doubts.”

4. Ibid.

Chapter 12

1. Paul David Tripp, *Suffering: Gospel Hope When Life Doesn’t Make Sense* (Wheaton, IL: Crossway, 2018), 96.

2. I originally shared these insights in my book *Pressure Points: A Guide to Navigating Student Stress* (Greensboro, NC: New Growth Press, 2019), 79.

3. These thoughts are originally from my book *Jacked: An Irrepressible Passion to Share the Gospel* (Orlando, FL: Cru Press, 2016), 21.

Conclusion

1. Timothy Keller, *The Meaning of Marriage: Facing the Complexities of Commitment with the Wisdom of God* (New York: Penguin, 2011), 116. Emphasis added.